4

THE ULSTER-SCOTS CLASSICS

BETSY GRAY

OR,

HEARTS OF DOWN:

A TALE OF NINETY-EIGHT.

W. G. LYTTLE

ULLANS PRESS

2008

First published in book form in 1888.

The text for this edition was taken from the undated 9th edition, published by Carswell of Belfast.

This reprint published by The Ullans Press 2008.

ISBN 1-905281-10-2

Cover illustration by Graham Kennedy

This drawing of Mat M'Clenaghan making pike heads in his smiddy at The Six Road Ends appeared on the cover of several of the earlier editions of this book.

PREFACE TO NINTH EDITION.

THIS story was originally written for and published in the columns of the North Down Herald. Its success was phenomenal, and the demand for its appearance in book form has been such as to warrant the issue of a very large edition. The incidents were collected from reliable sources ; relatives of the sufferers in '98 were interviewed, and the places written of were all visited by the author, who has, since the publication of the third edition gone to his well-earned rest. The present edition has been issued at the request of many persons, and to meet the still increasing demand.

CONTENTS.

CONTENTS

BETSY GRAY.

CHAPTER I.

THE SMIDDY AT THE SIX ROAD ENDS.

" Sworn helpers of the patriot band,
Who fight for home and fatherland,
Behold the brawny blacksmith's strike
With heavy, swift, and ringing blows,
As fierce the smiddy fire glows,
And fashion out the deadly pike." — LYTTLE

SIX roads unite in the townland of Granshaw, in the County of Down, at a point some two and a half miles from Bangor, three miles from Donaghadee, and a like distance from Newtownards. The place is commonly known as " The-Six-Road-Ends." Within a few hundred yards stands the palatial residence of Mr. James Knox, erected about the year 1880, and the country around is dotted with the comfortable but unpretentious homesteads of the industrious and thrifty farming population. The County Down Railway passes close to the spot, having a stopping place quite adjacent to it, called Groomsport Station. Beside it there are also a Presbyterian church and a post office.

Very few of the numerous persons who daily pass to and fro in the vicinity of the Six Road Ends are aware that in this quiet, peaceful, and picturesque neighbourhood, there once lived some of the bravest of the unfortunates of 1798, and that within a stone's cast of the junction of these roads stands the house in which was born the devoted, beautiful, and noble-hearted Betsy Gray, who headed the patriots at the Battle of Ballynahinch, whose beauty and bravery have been sung of by poets, whose chivalry has been recorded by historians, and whose memory is revered by countless thousands of the Irish people, irrespective of prejudice, politics, or religion.*

During the stirring events now to be related, and for many years prior thereto, there stood close to the Six Road Ends a cottier house and smiddy occupied by a blacksmith named Mat M'Clenaghan. The house and smiddy have long since disappeared, but the site upon which they stood is easily pointed out—a small field at the end of the Bangor Road, the property of Major Maxwell, and now occupied by a carpenter named Fletcher, and separated from the road by a low stone wall.

Mat M'Clenaghan was a decent, honest, hard-working fellow who had buried two wives and married a third. He was a prime favourite with his neighbours, could shoe a horse, make a harrow pin, or mend a plough with any man ; nor did his hard work debar him from joining in every local festivity, be it wedding or funeral, dance or wake—for in those days there was pretty nearly as much fun to be had at one of these occurrences as at the other. It was whispered that Mat was a United Irishman, and that his smiddy turned out more pikes than harrow pins ; but Mat was a cautious fellow, and though, as he shod a neighbour's horse, he could rattle off the gossip of the country for miles around, he was particularly reticent when chaffed by some people about the pikes, or when asked his opinion about the much talked of " rising. "

One dark night in October 1797, when the country people for miles around were wrapt in slumber, Mat's smiddy was the scene of life and bustle. The fire in his rude forge burned brightly, and, as a sturdy lad worked the huge bellows, a fierce flame shot upward, revealing the sinewy arms and grimy face of Mat as he worked by his anvil, and lighting up the black sooty walls of the interior of the building. The lurid glare of the forge

* Numerous writers have erroneously stated that Betsy Gray was a Killinchy lass, and a well-known poet, who penned some charming verses concerning this heroine, fell into the same error. He says :—

" If through Killinchy's woods and vales,
You searched a summer day,
The loveliest maiden to be found
Was bonnie Betsy Gray."

The writer of this story has traced the birth-place of Betsy Gray, and visited the house in which she lived. It stands within about two hundred yards of the mansion recently erected by Mr. James Knox, at Granshaw, Bangor, and is, at the period of writing, occupied by Mr. Hans Gray Macartney, a farmer, aged 80 years, whose mother was a cousin of Betsy's.

fire also discovered the presence of a visitor. Seated upon a large stone that lay upon the damp floor, and against the wall, sat a young man dressed in the plain working attire of a farmer. His face, as seen by the light of the smiddy fire, was singularly bold and handsome. He was of stout build, broad shouldered, and of middle height. He wore a soft felt hat, beneath which his long hair, of a soft brown colour, had the appearance of being neatly trimmed and well cared for. The visitor was George Gray. Now and then he would remove his hat, and, turning it round and round slowly between his hands, gaze into it attentively as though reading something hidden therein ; anon his eyes would follow the movements of Mat as, drawing a piece of red hot metal from the fire, he placed it upon his anvil, beating it out into a flat pointed blade, some twelve inches long, and plunged it with a hissing noise into a bucket of water that stood by his side. Mat was forging pikes. And the work seemed a pleasant one to him, for as he held the glowing metal in a pair of tongs by one hand and wielded his hammer with the other, a cloud of sparks leaping upwards and big drops of sweat rolling down his face—Mat sang away as merrily as though they were at a christening party or wedding festivity. High above the rude music of the anvil, and the roar of the furnace fire, was the rich bass voice of Mat M'Clenaghan as he carolled forth a favourite song of the period.

As Mat finished his song he swung the ponderous hammer round his head with a flourish, and flung it into a corner. Then turning to Gray he said—

" What's the metter, Geordie ? Why, there's no a word oot o' yer heid the nicht ava. "

George smiled sadly as he answered, " I do feel a bit dull, Mat, but I'll be all right in the morning. "

" Keep up yer heart, my boy," said Mat cheerily, as he slapped George on the back with his grimy hand, " the darkest hooer's aye afore daybrek, an' whun *we fin' the blackbird*—eh, Geordie ? "

" Ay, Mat, *when* we find it. "

Mat held up his finger and shook it reprovingly.

" Dinnae be throwin' a wat blanket on *me*, Geordie, acause if a didnae believe that everything wad gang richt, deil tak the pike I wad mak mair. "

" Well, you have made a good many, Mat," remarked George.

" Ay, ye may weel say that, if a man that a cud name seen what's hid in ' The Moat' he wad tell a gie story in a certain place."

" Whom do you mean, Mat ? "

" Wha dae a mean ? A'll tell ye that. " He paused and looked at the bellows-lad who stood with gaping mouth drinking in every word. Then stepping up to Gray's side he whispered a name in his ear.

It was the name of a suspected spy, whose doings will be disclosed in this tale.

George started.

" It's joking you are, Mat !" he exclaimed.

Mat turned to his assistant, saying—" Ye may gang awa tae yer bed, my boy ; we'll dae nae mair the nicht. "

As he spoke, Mat went to the smiddy door, and took down a stout iron cross bar which had held it fast. Then he cautiously stepped outside and listened. It was too dark for him to see a single object, and not a sound was heard save the sighing of the wintry wind as it swept through the leafless branches of some bushes that grew near Mat's dwelling. He stepped back into the smiddy, and at a sign from him the boy slipped out. Mat closed the door, replaced the bar, and sat down upon his anvil, facing George.

The latter was the first to speak. " What makes you think what you told me just now ?" he asked.

" It's mebbe mair a noshin o' my ain nor ocht else, " replied Mat. " He cums oot an' in here axin questins in a saft kin' o' a wae, but a turn on him quick sumtimes, whun he disnae expect me, like ; an' if ye seen his e'en then, ye wud sweer there wuz murder in his heart. "

" He's a man whom I would not have suspected, " said George, " but I shall watch him in future. I say, Mat, my sister Betsy has asked a few friends for tea next Wednesday evening, and she wants you to join us. "

" Wi' a' my heart! " exclaimed Mat. " Didn't the dear lady promise tae be at the krisnin' o' my wee boy the morrow nicht ; ah! Mester Geordie, a wud lay doon my life fur that bonnie sister o' yours. Tell her a'll be there. Wull a tak the fiddle wi' me ? "

" Better not, Mat ; it won't be a jolly tea party. Mr. Warwick will be over to give us full particulars about poor William Orr, of Antrim. "

The blacksmith clenched his huge fists. The fire had almost died out, but the light emitted from a large, dirty-looking tallow candle, that burned in an iron sconce driven into the wall, served to show the workings of Mat's features.

" Puir fella ! " he groaned ; " little did he deserve it. But he's in

Hevin this nicht, an' them that murdered him'll gang tae——"

Hush !" whispered George, holding up his hand, " I hear a step." The next moment there was a loud thump, as from a man's fist, upon the door.

" Wha's that ? " demanded Mat.

" A friend— James Dillon," was answered from without.

Mat darted a look full of meaning at George Gray. The name which he had whispered in George's ear was—" Jamey Dillon, o' Drumawhey."

Mat removed the iron bar, and opened the door. A man buttoned up in a huge frieze overcoat stepped into the smiddy.

CHAPTER II.

JAMES DILLON.

" Aye free aff han' yer story tell,
When wi' a bosom crony ;
But still keep something tae yersel'
Ye winnae tell tae ony ! "—BURNS.

DURING the brief moment which elapsed between the knock at the smiddy door and the opening of it by Mat M'Clenaghan, George Gray had taken the precaution of spreading an old sack over a quantity of pike heads that lay on the floor, where they had been thrown one by one as fashioned out at Mat's anvil.

The midnight visitor, dimly visible in the unsteady flare of the big tallow candle, was not prepossessing in appearance. He was a tall, thin man ; with hair, whiskers, and bushy eyebrows of a " sandy " or reddish colour. His visage was long, his nose broad, flat, and wide-nostrilled ; his lips thick and slightly protruding. His face, taken as a whole, while not absolutely ugly, had something repulsive about it, and the quick, ferret-like movements of his small grey watery eyes, as they goggled about beneath his shaggy beetling eyebrows, caused a feeling of unaccountable distrust or apprehension in the minds of most people with whom he associated.

As Dillon entered the smiddy he looked keenly at Mat, and remarked drily—

" You are late at work to-night, Mat. "

" That's naethin new, " was the quick reply, " a hadnae as thrang a saison this mony a year ; an' forbye that, a maun hae a' red up afore the krisnin, fur a daur say a'll hae a wheen days idle-set efter that."

Dillon darted a rapid glance around the smiddy, and, seeing George Gray standing against the wall, saluted him.

" Ah, Mr. Gray, " he said cordially, " is this where you are ? "

" Yes," answered George ; " Mat has a job on hands for me, and if I don't get it finished before this famous christening comes off, I needn't expect it sooner than Christmas. Like yourself, Mr. Dillon, I was out late, and hearing the sound of Mat's anvil, I stepped in to see how he was progressing."

Mat laughed.

" Ay, Geordie," he said, " you an' sum ither boys that a cud name ir oot late gie and affen. A ken what yer efter. That curly-heided lass at the Cottown wull lead ye a dance sum day. Man, but ye'll mak the purty pair. Mister Dillon, isn't it weel fur you an' me that haes oor coortin' days ower ?"

" I suppose it is, " answered Dillon ; " but Mat, you have had somewhat more than your share of courting."

" Am no badly aff," laughed Mat ; " this wife's the third yin, an' a might hae twa or three mair afore a dee."

Dillon turned to George Gray, and said—

" You have heard the news confirmed about Orr, of Antrim ? "

" I have," replied George, in a grave voice ; " he was a worthy man, and has been unjustly executed."

" *Executed !* " exclaimed Mat, as he tugged at the strings of his leather apron to loose them, " *murdered*, ye mean ! "

Dillon gave a low whistle.

" Strong language, Mat," he said ; you are a rash man, and that tongue of yours will get you into trouble some day. Take care, Mat, take care ! "

" A cannae help speekin' what a think," was the surly answer. " It's cumin' noo that nae man's life wull be safe at the han's o' his nixt daur neibor."

" I hope it will never come to that," put in George.

" I trust not," said Dillon ; " but take my word for it we live in stirring times, and before we are much older the hangman's office will be a paying one ."

George shuddered.

" Heaven help the oppressed, Mr. Dillon," he said ; " this old country of ours would be the happiest, the brightest, and the most contented spot in all God's universe, if our rulers would but do her justice and treat her fairly."

" An' ye'll niver get jistis till ye fecht fur it wi' pike an' gun," cried the impetuous and hot-headed blacksmith.

George threw him a warning look.

" And in my opinion," said Dillon, " the pike and gun will only serve to make matters worse than they are. Agitate and petition as you will, but if you rise up in armed rebellion you will find it to be a black day for Ireland."

" An' a bluidy yin, " laughed Mat, nothing daunted.

" Yes, and a bloody one," echoed Dillon.

George Gray evidently did not relish the turn which the conversation had taken. He made a motion as though about to leave, and addressing Mat, said—

" I'll be over at the christening in good time, Mat."

" I had quite forgotten that affair," said Dillon ; " when does it come off ? "

" The morrow nicht, " replied Mat.

" I suppose you'll have a big gathering," said Dillon.

" The hoose disnae haud mony folk, but it wull be gie an' fu' ye may be shair," was Mat's answer.

" I don't think you sent me an invitation, " said Dillon, in a bantering tone.

A frown gathered on Mat's grimy face ; it was momentary, however, and escaped Dillon's eye. Then he said, with a strong effort to appear cordial—

" Weel, Mester, a dinnae ken hoo a cud forget *you*. Come wi' the rest o' the fowk an' mak yersel' welkim."

" Thank you, Mat," said Dillon ; " who will be the clergyman ? "

" His reverince Mister Steele Dickson," was the quick reply.

" Steele Dickson !" exclaimed Dillon, with a look of astonishment ; " what on earth do you bring him to baptise your child for ? "

" Acause a like him," said Mat.

" But he is not your minister ; you go to the Rev. James M'Cullough, of Newtownards ; and look at the distance you bring Mr. Dickson— from Portaferry all the way."

" A had a sittin' frae him whun he preeched in Ballyhalbert," said Mat, " an' a niver likit ony meinister sae well. He krisined a' my waens."

Dillon gave a short, dry cough, and fixed his ferret eyes sharply on Mat's face. There was a moment's silence, and then Dillon said —

" I confess I don't admire your choice."

" He's a cliver man, " said Mat sharply.

" He is," said Dillon, " and he's more than that. People say he's a rebel and a Papist at heart ! "

Mat fired up, heedless of the warning looks of George Gray.

" A Papist ! " he shouted ; that's aye the cry. A wush a wuz as guid as sum of them ; it wud be tellin' me. A dinnae care a thraneen what a man's religion is sae as he is honest an' his heart in the richt place. A suppoas sum fowk wud only let Presbyterians intil Heaven."

Mat was fast getting angry, and George Gray was growing decidedly uneasy. Dillon alone seemed happy and at ease. He appeared determined to follow up the subject, as he said—

" Mat you're a shrewd, sensible fellow ; you have heard Dickson preach ; you have heard his speeches, and you know the sort of man he is. He took the United Irishman's oath seven years ago ; some people say that he's a *rebel*, and that hanging is too good for him."

At this juncture George Gray interposed.

" Mr. Dillon, " he said, " the hour is late and we should all be in our beds. Discussions of this kind are unpleasant and your remarks are evidently displeasing to Mat's kindly nature. "

" I am sorry if I have said a word to offend you, Mat, " said Dillon, with an assumed frankness.

" Oh, it's a' richt " said Mat ; " a'm mebbe no as near Heaven as ither fowk, but a'll aye tak a freen's pert. It's six-an'-twunty year since a first seen Mister Dickson at Ballyhalbert, an' a niver knowed him tae be ocht else but a God-fearin' man an' a gentleman."

" Well, well, Mat, I didn't say anything against him."

" Ye did," said Mat fiercely ; " ye ca'd him a Papish an' a rebel ! "

" No, Mat, you wrong me ; I merely remarked *that people said so*. Am I not correct, Mr. Gray ? "

" I dare say you are, " said George, drily. " And possibly you are aware what gave rise to the rumour on idle gossips' tongues that Mr. Dickson was a Papist at heart ? "

" No, I am not aware," said Dillon.

" Then I'll tell you," said Gray ; " the maiden name of the parish priest's mother was Dickson. That fact furnished a peg sufficiently strong for some people to hang their hats on."

What more might have followed it is hard to say, had not the candle burned down close to its iron socket, and now spluttered and flared in its expiring efforts. Mat opened the door of the smiddy, and the three stepped out into the cold, moist air. The blacksmith placed the hasp of the door upon the iron staple which was driven into the door post ; then he adjusted the padlock and turned the key.

" Well, Mat, good-night," said Dillon.

" Good-night," said Mat.

" Good-night, George."

" Good-night, Mr. Dillon."

The next moment Dillon was walking towards his home in Drumawhey. When his footsteps died in the distance, George said to Mat—

" Be on your guard, Mat ; I share your opinions *now* regarding that man."

" A can see as far through a milestane as my neibors," replied Mat.

Then they parted ; George to revolve in his mind certain plans for the future, and Mat to kiss the sleeping babe which was to be lionised on the morrow, and to enjoy the repose which he had earned by his heavy labour. For him the future had no dread of danger. The land in which he dwelt was about to be deluged in blood ; deeds were on the eve of perpetration the bare mention of which would appal the stoutest heart. Mat recked not of those things ; his only concern just now was lest the " krisnin " might not prove the jolliest one ever held at the Six-Road-Ends. He had done his best to make it a success, and I shall now invite all my readers to the interesting ceremony of a County Down christening in the olden time.

CHAPTER III.

THE CHRISTENING.

" My ain pet ! my honey doo ! my troutie o' the burn !
Sair, sair ye keep yer mammy back frae daein' mony a turn !
O fond's the look yer daddy tak's, as guiless ye lie there
Chasin' frae his honest broo mony a dowie care !
Baloo ! my bairnie fa' asleep ! O hushy, hushy, ba ! "—SMITH.

A HUGE turf fire blazed upon the broad, pleasant hearth of Mat M'Clenaghan. Turf was plenty in those days, and the Granshaw moss gave promise of holding out for centuries to come. Mat's good wife Isabel, or " Bel " as she was called, was alive to the fact that nothing contributes more to the cheerful aspect of a home than a bright fire ; and so, thrifty and frugal though she was, she built up the peats with unsparing hand upon the glowing pile until the atmosphere of the kitchen was like that of a bakehouse. The earthen floor, smooth, hard and shining, was clean as heather besom could make it ; every article of tinware upon the walls might have served as a looking glass ; the wooden dresser was fresh and white ; everything in the house had the appearance of absolute cleanliness.

A clumsy wooden cradle stood in one corner, near to the fire, and in it there reposed the youngest of the M'Clenaghan's. Ever and anon would the kindly mother pause in her household duties to gaze upon the face of her little one, and murmur a blessing upon the sleeping infant.

" A'm sayin", Bel, wuz onybuddy tuchin' my razer ? "

It was the voice of Mat, strong and sonorous, from the adjoining room, where he was preparing his outward man for the approaching ceremony.

" Wheest, man or ye'll wauken up the waen !" was the woman's reply, as she hurried to the room door.

Mat was in a temper. His face was plentifully lathered with soap ; from one side of his chin the blood was flowing freely, and he held up the razor so that his wife might examine the condition of its edge.

" Waen, dear ye hae cut yersel'," she murmured sympathetically.

" Cut mysel' ! Weel, a think a hae ; mebbe a'll bleed till daith. Get me a cobwab, fast ! "

Darting her hand under a table, Bel fumbled about the corners of it, and straightway produced a supply of cobwebs which she deftly clapped upon Mat's bleeding chin.

Mat was a good soul, but easily put out of sorts. Some of his young people had evidently been whittling sticks with his razor—not too good a one at the best—and he sat down to have a look at it before resuming operations.

" Wull a get ye the strap, dear ? " asked his wife.

" Wull ye get me the strap ?" echoed Mat, half angrily, half jestingly ; " A may tak it oot tae the anvil an' pit an edge on it wi' the sledge, an' efter that mebbe a rub on a scythe stane micht be usefu' tae it."

While he was talking Bel had drawn a big jar from under the bed. A twinkle of Mat's eye and a droll twitching of the corners of his mouth showed that he understood her intentions fully, but he kept rattling away until the good woman handed him a tumbler containing a liberal glass of liquor drawn from the jar.

" What's that ? " demanded Mat, as yet in a very bad humour.

" Jest a wee taste o' what a niver seen ye refusin' yit," replied Bel. " Tak it up, dear ; it'll studdy yer han' an' mebbe stap the bleedin'. "

Mat needed no pressing. He laid down the offending razor, and

"Are you able to hold up your child, Matthew?"
See Page 13.

took the tumbler from his wife's hand.

" Here's tae ye, Bel," he cried, laughingly, and tossed off the whiskey.

" It'll tak a lang time tae owertak the first yin, Mat, " said Bel.

" Ay, wuman, ye niver spauk a truer wurd, " he answered. " A hae drunk as muckle whusky as wud fill the big dam. "

" Deed, Mat, ye maun quat it," said his wife. " A wud rether see ye bringin' in a bag o' Inglis's flooer than a jar o' whusky ony day."

" Blethers, wuman ! " laughed Mat ; " why, there's mair fun in yin jur o' whusky than in a kert load o' Inglis's flooer ! "

" That may a' be, dear," was Bel's reply ; " like iverything else, whuskey's very guid sae long as ye keep it in its richt place an' dinnae abuse it."

" An' a'm the very boy kens its richt place, an' pits it intil it," laughed Mat. Then, as he held out his tumbler, he added in a wheedling voice—

" Here, Bel, jest gie me anither, an' then a'll quat."

But the jar had been replaced under the bed, and the frugal housewife was unwilling to replenish the tumbler.

" Ye hae got eneuch the noo," she urged.

" Just yin mair tae keep the tither company," said Mat, " a'm shair a bird cannae flee wi' yin wing."

It is needless to say that Bel yielded, as every dutiful wife should, to her husband's wishes. Mat forgot his bleeding face ; a few strokes upon his hone made the razor all right ; his face was soon cleanly shaven ; he donned his Sunday attire, and half-an-hour later stood at the door of his cottage ready to bid welcome to his expected guests. Mat had a quick eye and a far-seeing one. That keen eye of his swept the various roads that branched off from his dwelling, and as certain human figures came in view, he turned to his wife, crying merrily—

" They're cumin', Bel ; here they ir ! Is the glesses reddy ? An' the boilin' water an' the whusky, and sumthin' saft for the lasses, to wit, that world-famed beverage, ' Sedna,' prepared by Deans, Logan & Co., Ltd., Belfast. Oh, powers o' war, but this wull be a day an' a nicht ! Shair it's mebbe the last krisnin we'll hae, wuman, so the deil tak expense ! "

It was astonishing how many people Mat M'Clenaghan was able to pack into that small house of his. Young and old were there, but the latter predominated. They sat in the kitchen and in the sleeping apartment also, or " doon the hoose," as it was then and still is termed in County Down. The guests began to arrive in the early part of the afternoon, but these were chiefly the elder of the females, who came to give Mrs. M'Clenaghan a hand at making the needful preparations, and to attend to the wants and necessities of the younger people.

Mat was in his glory, and one to see and hear him might have supposed him to be the owner of broad acres, instead of the poor, hard-working, hard-fisted blacksmith of the Six-Road-Ends. But in his heart happiness reigned supreme, and he would not have changed lots with the proudest in the land.

Close to the blazing turf fire sat Biddy Brown, who filled the dual office of nurse and midwife for miles around. Her white cap and blue and white checked apron were spotlessly clean, and her face wore that look of quiet contentment and grave responsibility so often to be seen with persons of her profession. On her knee slept the infantile M'Clenaghan, robed in a snow-white dress, neatly embroidered, decked out for its baptismal ceremonial.

Mat attended to one duty and that alone. It was the distribution of the whiskey. Every one had a tumbler either in hand or near at hand, and as Mat every now and then replenished a jug from the big jar, before referred to, and went from one to another tendering a fresh supply, it was amusing to hear the various remarks made to and by his guests.

" Noo, Mistress M'Callister," Mat would say, " divil the drap ye hae tuk frae yer gless since a pit the first hauf yin in it."

" Agh, Mat dear, this is twa or three times ye hae helpit me ; it is, as true as daith, an' a maun not tak ony mair."

" Launey, launey, Mat dear," another would exclaim, " dinnae offer me ony mair ; that's Cruiskeen Lawn a'm shair, fur a fin' it in my heid already."

And thus it went round. Some protested, yet, even as they did so, held out their glasses for a fresh supply ; others really meant what they said and refused to indulge further.

" Agh, Biddy, we mauna forget you," exclaimed Mat, as he approached the nurse and replenished her glass ; " what dae ye think o' that waen, Biddy ? "

" A nicer yin niver cummed intae the wurl, " replied Biddy, as she softly kissed the sleeping baby. " An' may it be a blissin' til its da and ma, an' a credit tae the auld cuntry. "

" Sae be it," responded nearly all present.

" Weel, Biddy, ye ocht tae be a judge, " cried the proud parent, " acause ye hae pit a guid wheen o' them throo yer han's this last fifty years, an' noo a'll tell ye yin an' a' what a'm gaun tae mak o' that boy ye see there—"

What Mat would have said remained unspoken, for at that moment a hand was laid upon the latch, the door opened, and he who had been chosen to bestow upon the child its name entered the humble habitation.

Every one rose in respectful silence as the Rev. William Steele Dickson stepped into the cottage. He was a man of fine physique and commanding presence : a clergyman whose fame as a preacher and orator had reached the remotest parts of County Down, and who was beloved for his genial manner, his high character, and his remarkable benevolence.

" Good evening to you all," he said, as he stepped forward to shake the hand of Mrs. M'Clenaghan ; and then he had a warm grasp and a kindly word for every one.

Half an hour was passed in general conversation, and then preparations were made for the christening. Poor Mat was in a condition far from suitable to the occasion. His frequent applications to the brown jug were beginning to tell upon him. There was a glitter in his eye and an unsteadiness in his gait which were not in keeping with his position and the duties which he would be called upon to discharge.

Mr. Dickson read a portion of Scripture and offered up a prayer. Then he asked to have the child brought forward. At this stage a series of nudges went round the company, and not a few had difficulty in restraining their laughter as they noted the tremendous efforts made by Mat to appear sober and solemn. His condition did not escape the keen, observant eye of the clergyman, and there was just the faintest sign of twitching about the corners of his mouth as he lifted the babe, and placing it in the arms of its father, said—

" Are you able to hold up your child, Matthew ? "

"Am a what ?" said Mat ; " able tae haud it up ! Ay, Mister Dickson, that a em, if it wuz the wecht o' a twa year auld stirk ! "

This was more than the assembly could stand ; there was a titter of laughter, and then the merriment, which could not be restrained, burst forth. Even the clergyman could not refrain from smiling and it was evident that he had much difficulty in maintaining the solemnity befitting the occasion.

All went well until Mr. Dickson sprinkled some drops of cold water upon the face of the sleeping infant. The effect was electrical. The sleeper awoke instantly and uttered a piercing wail. Mat turned fiercely on Biddy the nurse, and once more utterly upset the gravity of all present by saying, in a deep whisper—

" Dang saze ye, Biddy, why didn't ye tak the deid cauld aff the water ! "

It was all over at last. Mr Dickson delivered his charge to the parents, after the custom of the Church to which he belonged ; and, apologising for his inability to remain and partake of their hospitality, he took his leave and turned his steps towards the residence of Betsy Gray.

" God gang wi' ye ! " cried Mat, as soon as his reverence was beyond earshot. " God gang wi' ye ! A niver feel richt at mysel whun there's a meinister in the hoose. Come Bel, toss up the taythings, an' let us hae sumthin tae eat."

Bel did as she was desired. A large table, drawn into the centre of the kitchen, was quickly laden with home-baked bread of various kinds, oat-cake, potato cake, pancakes, soda-cake, and other manufactures. Cheese, butter, eggs, and jam were in abundance, and such as could obtain a seat were soon at work. It was impossible to accommodate all the company at the table, so many of them were obliged to hold their teacups in their hands, much after the fashion of a drawing-room tea at the present day.

Many were the subjects touched on in conversation, but chief among them were the condition of the country and the probability of an early " rising."

" Did ye hear about Jock Smiley bein' feered tae join the United Irishmen ? " asked Mat.

" Na, " cried several ; " dae tell us a' aboot it. "

" Weel, ye ken Jock's no jist a' there, " said Mat, putting his finger significantly to his forehead, " so sumbuddy shewed him a pike yin day an' tell't him that wuz the waipin the boys wud hae to fecht wi' yin o' these days. Weel, Jock cummed forrit tae tak the oath, as wuz thocht ; but he stud a wee minit, an' sez he—' A cannae dae it.' ' Ye cannae dae what ? ' they axed him. ' A cannae join ye,' sez Jock, ' fur a hae seen them pikes yer gaun tae fecht wi', an' a jag frae yin o' them wud be hell ! ' "

There was a shout of laughter at this which drowned the rattling of cups and the clatter of spoons. But above the din was heard the voice of Mat's wife, as she exclaimed—

" Haud yer tongues, waens, here's Miss Betsy Gray."

CHAPTER IV.

BETSY GRAY.

" If through Killinchy's woods and vales
You searched a summer day,
The loveliest maiden to be found
Was bonnie Betsy Gray." — M'COMB

NUMEROUS Irish historians describe Betsy Gray as a native of Killinchy and as the joy and pride of a widowed mother. Both statements are erroneous. She was born, as I have already said, at Granshaw, quite close to the Six-Road-Ends. Her mother died before the troubles of '98, but her father was alive. He was a farmer, in very comfortable circumstances, widely known and respected throughout North Down. He fairly doated upon his daughter Betsy. She was his only daughter, and he lavished upon her the wealth of his great heart's love. Unwilling that she should take any part in farm or household drudgery, Mr. Gray sent his daughter to a ladies' school where she received a high-class education. She had now reached her twentieth year, and was possessed of wondrous beauty, a beauty enriched and enhanced by a warm heart, an ardent temperament and lady-like accomplishments. Her beauty and her goodness formed a theme for every tongue wherever she went and many a wealthy suitor sought her hand in marriage.

Such was the visitor who now stepped into Mat M'Clenaghan's cottage, leaning upon the arm of her brother George.

" What wae ir ye, Miss Betsy ? " cried Mat, stepping to meet her, and maintaining his equilibrium as well as he could.

" Thanks, Mat, I am very well," and then having said a few words to the company, she advanced to the nurse and took the little baby boy in her arms.

" The dear little man, " she murmured, kissing the infant's velvet cheek, " the dear little man ! Your own image, Mat, I assure you."

" Thank ye, Miss, " exclaimed Mat, proud of the compliment, " but a hope he'll be a wiser and a better man. "

" He is in God's hands, " said Betsy seriously. " He it was who sent him here for some wise purpose, and He alone knows what the future has in store for him."

" True, Miss Betsy, very true," said Mat's wife, " but pit the waen doon an' tak a cup o' tay."

Betsy restored the old nurse her charge and sat down to the humble feast. There was nothing in her presence or manner to awe her humbler neighbours, or to make them feel uncomfortable : on the contrary, her presence, like sunlight, seemed to gladden every heart and brighten up the humble cot.

By and by the tea cups were removed, and a kind of fireside concert was commenced. Mat was chief contributor, but his songs were always welcome. The following one met with a very hearty reception :—

Once on a morning of sweet recreation,
I heard a fair lady a-making her moan,
With sighing and sobbing, and sad lamentation,
Aye singing, " My Blackbird for ever is flown !
He's all my heart's treasure, my joy, and my pleasure !
So justly my love, my heart follows thee ;
And I am resolved, in fair or foul weather,
To seek out my Blackbird, wherever he be.

" I will go, a stranger to peril and danger.
My heart is so loyal in every degree ;
For he's constant and kind and courageous in mind,
Good luck to my Blackbird, wherever he be !
In Scotland he's loved and dearly approved,
In England a stranger he seemeth to be,
But his name I'll advance, in Ireland or France
Good luck to my Blackbird, wherever he be !

" The birds of the forest are all met together,
The turtle is chosen to dwell with the dove,
And I am resolved in fair or foul weather,
Once in the springtime to seek out my love.
But since fickle fortune, which still proves uncertain,
Hath caused this parting betwixt him and me,
His right I'll proclaim, and who dares me blame ?
Good luck to my Blackbird, wherever he be ! "

" What do you mean by the blackbird, Mat ? " asked Betsy smiling demurely.

" Agh, Miss Betsy, ye ken richt weel athoot axin'," said Mat.

" I suppose you hope to find it some day," pursued Betsy.

" Heth a dae," replied Mat, " an' afore twa springs is ower, a hope."

" I hope so, too," said the lady, with much fervour.

As the night wore on the older people slipped away to their homes. Not so with the younger folk, who were determined to make a night of it. Tables, chairs, and stools were piled against the walls, and some of them carried into the smiddy. The kitchen floor thus cleared, Mat took down his fiddle from the wall and struck up a lively reel. There was a scramble for partners as though the eager dancers feared that a single stroke of Mat's bow would be lost, and at it they went. The fiddling was not so classic and finished as that of a Paganini or a Cohen, nor the dancing so graceful as that of modern schools, but they all did their best. Mat rasped away, and every now and then, uttered a " hoogh ! " which could be heard above the noise of the stamping feet upon the earthen floor.

Gayest amongst the gay was our lovely heroine. Fitted by nature and education to grace the most brilliant assemblages, she was far happier amongst those honest but warm-hearted people, for they had grown up together and a bond of affection united them. Such dancing was tiresome work, and after a while it gave place to household games, many of which are still practised. It was during the progress of these that Willie Boal of the Cottown and James Dillon of Drumawhey entered—two men who are to take very prominent positions in the remarkable events which are to be recorded in this story.

Dillon sat down beside Mat to drink the health of the youngster ; Willie Boal stole up to Betsy and sat down by her side, pressing her hand warmly as he did so.

" You are late, Willie," said Betsy.

" Yes, Betsy, I am ; I meant to be here earlier."

Then he lapsed into silence.

Betsy regarded him for some moments, and then enquired :

" Has anything troubled you, Willie ? You seem dull."

" Yes," replied Boal ; something has reached my knowledge which causes me anxiety. When did you see our friend, Mr. Warwick ? "

" Not for some time," responded Betsy ; " but he is expected to be at my father's house on Wednesday night. Why do you ask ? "

" He has offended Dillon in some way. Tell him to be cautious. But hush ! Here comes Dillon this way."

CHAPTER V.

UNWELCOME VISITORS.

" The sodgers ir comin' ! rin fast! rin fast !
Wi' guns an' wi' baynets ! rin fast ! rin fast !
They're lukin' fur guns, an' they're lukin fur pikes,
They'll show ye nae mercy, the bloodthirsty tykes ! "—OLD SONG.

THE door of Mat M'Clenaghan's cottage was thrown violently open, and Tommy Burns, the lad who worked with Mat at the forge in the smiddy, dashed in, pale, excited and breathless.

" What's wrang ?" cried several.

" The sodgers ! " he gasped ; " they're comin' !"

In a moment all was confusion, and the utmost consternation prevailed. Some prepared to fly, but wiser counsels prevailed, and it was suggested by George Gray, whose coolness and self-possession never forsook him for an instant, that a dance should be begun, as the soldiers, finding them thus engaged, would in all probability depart in peace. Besides, as he said, the visit might not be intended for them.

But Mat, the fiddler, had disappeared. Repeated doses of Cruiskeen whiskey had completely upset him ; he was stretched on the bed which stood in the adjoining room, and his snoring was distinctly audible in the kitchen.

" Give me the fiddle quick ! " cried Willie Boal ; " come lads, choose your partners ! "

It was the work of a moment. Gaily rasped the fiddle and quickly flew the feet of the dancers, but their hearts throbbed painfully, and many a cheek was deadly white.

The suspense was terrible, but it was of short duration.

The door, which Tommy had closed and barred behind him, was burst open, and a military officer, followed by half a dozen soldiers, filed into the kitchen.

The dancers stood suddenly still.

" What's going on here ? " demanded the leader, in an insolent tone.

" A krisenin," someone replied.

" A what ? " queried the officer.

Here poor Bel M'Clenaghan pressed forward, wringing her hands.

" A krisenin, indeed, indeed, sir," she sobbed ; " my ain waen, sir, an' there it is in its wee cradle."

The man looked puzzled.

" Stop your dammed gibberish !" he exclaimed, " and tell me what you mean."

As he spoke he darted a rapid glance round the assemblage, and his eye instantly singled out Betsy Gray.

" Oh, ho !" he chuckled. " A winsome jade, upon my soul ! Do you clatter in this infernal jargon, madam, or can you tell why these people are here ? "

" I can, sir," said Betsy.

" Then be pleased to do so," said the soldier in a voice less harsh, and bowing stiffly to the beautiful girl.

With a flush upon her cheek, but in a voice that never quivered, Betsy spake—

" The occupants of this house are Mat M'Clenaghan, his wife, and family. This afternoon the youngest child has been baptised. We (waving her hand round the assembled guests) are their neighbours, and have been celebrating the event by a dance. Such is the custom of the country."

" Well spoken, my pretty lass," said the officer, in a wheedling tone ; " sorry I haven't time to try a step with you ; but, by my faith, I have time to kiss so sweet a mouth at any rate ! "

As he spoke he attempted to throw his arm round Betsy's waist. Quick as lightning Betsy drew back, and at the same instant her brother and Willie Boal stepped between her and the amorous officer.

" Pardon me, sir ! " said George Gray. " Your errand here surely cannot be to offer insult to a lady."

" Who the devil are you, sir ? " cried the officer, laying his hand on his sword and eyeing George angrily.

" I am this lady's brother," replied George, " and shall resent any insult offered to her. Keep your sword in its scabbard ! "

George stood in the glare of the candles and of the blazing fire, drawn up to his full height. There was a dangerous gleam in his eyes, and the heaving of his broad chest showed how deeply he was moved.

The officer eyed him fixedly for a few moments, then suddenly asked—

" Your name, fellow ? "

" George Gray," was the answer.

The officer took a memorandum book from his pocket and noted down the name.

" Where do you live ? "

" Quite close to this—in Granshaw."

" Your name ? " demanded the intruder, turning to George's friend.

" William Boal," was the steady answer, " and I live at Cottown."

" Now, where's M'Clenaghan ? " shouted the soldier, turning round fiercely.

" In bed, sir," said Mat's wife, now sobbing piteously.

" Stop your blubbering, damn you ! " was the rude rejoinder. " Show me the bed."

" A wull, sir ; cum doon this wae," said Bel, making ineffectual efforts to suppress her sobs.

She took up a candle and led the way to the bedroom, followed by the officer and two soldiers. The other four guarded the door of the apartment.

At a sign from the leader one of the soldiers took the candle from Bel's hand and held it close to Mat's face.

He was sound asleep, lying upon his back.

" What ails him ? " demanded the officer.

" Agh, sir, he's jist been takin' a drap ower muckle on accoont o' the krisnin," sobbed the affrighted woman ; " but shair yer honner's no wantin' ocht wi' my Mat ? "

" I want to ask him a few questions, and I don't believe he's a bit drunk," was the reply.

Then, seizing Mat by the collar, he shook him violently, and shouted:

" Get up, will you ! "

" A'll no change my liquor," muttered the sleeping man ; " anither half yin jist tae keep the tithers company."

One of the soldiers laughed. He appeared to understand the dialect, and also to fully comprehend Mat's condition. The officer looked at him.

" Dead drunk, sir ! " said the soldier, saluting his superior.

" Shake him up ! " said the leader, savagely.

The man put down his musket and laid hold of Mat. He shook him vigorously, but as well might he have shaken the bed on which Mat lay. Wake him he could not.

The officer turned to his men—

" Jones ! " he said.

" Yes, sir ! "

" You and Berkley keep guard ; let the others search the house ! "

" Yes, sir ! "

" Search the house, sir ! " cried Bel, falling upon her knees and wringing her hands wildly. " What dae ye want tae search my hoose fur ? "

" For arms—for pikes," was the answer.

Poor Bel was horror stricken. Springing to her feet, she flung her arms round Mat's neck, and cried wildly—

" Oh, Mat, Mat ! Wauken up, dear ! Wauken up, fur the sojers ir here lukin' fur pikes."

But Mat snored louder than ever.

Then from the kitchen a shrill voice was heard shouting—

" Let me go ! There's nae pikes here a tell ye ! "

" What's all this ? " demanded the officer, striding into the kitchen.

He found one of his men holding Tommy Burns by the arms. The boy was struggling to free himself, and he kicked and bit the soldier wickedly.

" Be quiet, boy, or I'll slice your head off ! " cried the officer drawing his sword and flashing it across Tommy's eyes.

The sight of the glittering blade had the desired effect. Tommy stood silent and motionless.

" Who is this boy ? " asked the officer.

Some one explained that Tommy assisted Mat at his work in the smiddy.

" Then the chances are he can save us the trouble of a search, and I don't wish to be kept here all night," said the officer.

Taking the lad by the collar, he demanded—

" Where does your master keep the pikes ? "

" Pikes ! " said the boy with well-feigned astonishment ; " what's pikes ? "

" The devil ! " muttered his questioner ; then in a loud tone—

" Your master makes pikes ? "

" Diz he ? " asked Tommy with a vacant stare.

" You know he does—tell the truth," said the officer, growing angry.

" A ken he maks harrow pins," said the lad ; that's a' that a ken."

" We'll find means to make you tell," said the officer, sheathing his sword. " Here, lads, bring him out."

George Gray stepped forward.

" You do not mean to harm the boy, do you ? " he asked.

The officer turned sharply upon him.

" How does that concern you ? " he demanded.

" He is a mere child." urged George, " you can have no authority to molest him."

" Mind your own business, young man," was the curt reply ; " I have authority to do just as I like in these matters, and mark me, sir, if you further attempt to obstruct me in the discharge of my duty, I shall place you under arrest."

George's eyes flashed, and a hot reply rose to his lips. It was checked by his sister Betsy, who placed her hand upon his arm and whispered—

" Don't, George. "

Suddenly a thought seemed to strike the soldier who had been addressed as Jones. Saluting his officer, he pointed to the cradle and said—

" The pikes may be there, sir ! "

" Look, " said the officer, with a nod of approval.

The soldier instantly obeyed ; with one hand he rudely thrust aside old Biddy, who was moaning loudly and rocking the cradle ; with the other he plucked the coverlet from off the child.

" Oh, my waen ! dinnae touch my waen ! " shrieked the infant's mother, as she pushed the soldier aside and flung herself across the cradle to shield her babe from harm.

So sudden was the push she gave the soldier, and so vigorous, that he staggered against the fire-place and all but fell upon the blazing pile of turf. He recovered himself in a moment.

" Damn you for a hag ! " he shouted, seizing her by the hair, which had fallen down her shoulders, and giving her a violent pull, he flung her upon the floor. She struck the ground with a dull, heavy thud. The next instant she was in the arms of Betsy Gray and several other friends.

The officer laughed, and stood looking on, biting his moustache and evidently enjoying the scene.

The soldier was a brute, and his brutish nature was aroused. Seizing the unconscious babe by its feet, he lifted it from the cradle, and swung it clear round his head.

A shriek of horror burst from the by-standers.

" The rebel brat ! " shouted the enraged soldier, " will I dash its brains out, sir ? "

Betsy Gray sprang forward and caught the child.

" Monster !" she gasped, " would you harm a helpless infant ? "

The soldier glared at her like a wild beast thirsting for blood.

" Hold, Jones ! " said the officer, stepping forward. " I am in the humour to gratify this young woman. Give her the brat."

The soldier relinquished his hold of the now screaming child, and lifting the cradle, tossed the contents of it upon the floor.

There were no pike heads there !

The man looked at his leader with an air of disappointment.

" Never mind, Jones," said that worthy, " we shan't march from Newton and back without some fun. Here, bring this stubborn lad outside."

Jones and one of his comrades laid violent hands upon poor Tommy, but the boy never quailed for an instant.

George Gray and Willie Boal would have interfered, but Betsy's pleading looks restrained them, and they still hoped that the soldiers would not proceed to violence.

" I'll give you one more chance," said the officer, facing the blacksmith's lad and looking fiercely into his eyes. " Where are the pikes ? "

" A dinnae ken ! " was the boy's stolid answer.

" Out with him ! " said the officer.

The two soldiers dragged the unresisting lad out of doors.

Every inmate of the house followed, men and women, pressing closely upon the soldiers. Other forms were seen moving about in the neighbourhood of the building, and the clank of arms told the affrighted people that the house was surrounded by soldiery.

" Stand back ! " shouted the officer, drawing his sword and waving it round his head. " I warn you," he continued, " that if you offer the slightest interference I shall order my men to fire on you. Their muskets are loaded with ball ! "

The people drew back. The women sobbed. The men uttered bitter curses—not loud but deep.

" Get lights ! " shouted the leader.

But the men had anticipated his orders. From Mat's yard they had brought a quantity of turf and bog fir. These they piled up just at the centre of the Six-Road-Ends and applied a light.

Merrily blazed the pile ! Little did honest Mat's neighbours think when they drew him home his winter's firing that it was to be applied to so fiendish a purpose.

But another chapter is required for a description of one of those savage deeds of wanton cruelty which roused the indignation of the world, and incited the Patriots of Ireland to rush to arms, that upon the field of battle they might avenge the wrongs of years.

CHAPTER VI.

A CRUEL DEED.

" Ay, ye may do your worst ! " he cried ;
" My very heart strings ye may sever,
Remember Orr ! for us he died—
Shall I be an informer ? Never ! "—LYTTLE.

MERRILY blazed the pile ! If the lads and lasses who loiter by the Six-Road-Ends at close of day, sitting upon the low stone wall which bounds Mat M'Clenaghan's field, or lounging against the fragrant hedgerows, could but look back to the scene enacted there that dark October night in 1797, what a thrill of horror would pass through every heart !

Merrily blazed the pile ! A cloud of smoke, a sheet of flame shot upward, while in the near distance the darkness seemed like a huge circular wall piled up around the soldiery and the people. Just at the roadside was a gate, leading to Mat's house. It hung on two stout posts of bog oak, rugged and undressed. As the leader of the soldiers surveyed the scene his eye fell upon the gate posts.

" This will do ! " he shouted. " Here, Jones, you and Jenkins strip the fellow and tie him to one of those gate posts."

" Yes, sir," was the ready response, and the next moment Tommy was in the rude hands of the ruffians, who quickly divested him of his jacket, vest and shirt, leaving the lad exposed to the biting winter wind, stripped of all but his ragged trousers.

The fellows knew their work, and they did it quickly. In less than five minutes from the order had been given, Tommy Burns was tied by a stout cord to the gate post. The blaze of the fire revealed the face of the lad as plainly as the light of day. It was ghastly pale, and there was a pleading look in his eyes as they were turned now on his tormentors and anon upon his friends, who were powerless to help him.

" Oh, George ! " sobbed Betsy, " what do they mean to do ? This is horrible."

" Come with me, Betsy," whispered George, taking his sister by the arm.

The girl yielded unresistingly. George led her back to Mat's house, and placing her in a chair took her by the hand. She repeated her question—" George, dear, what do they mean to do ? " But ere her brother could answer there arose from without a shriek so shrill, so full of mortal agony, that the blood curdled in the listeners' veins.

" Curse them ! " groaned George, " they are flogging the lad." He covered his face with his hands, and Betsy, dropping her head upon his shoulder, burst into a fit of weeping.

Ay, they were flogging him !

In those days the soldiers carried with them their instruments of torture, and woe betide the unfortunate creatures who provoked their wrath.

The soldier who had been bitten by Tommy begged to be permitted to wield the lash, and permission was most readily given. With clenched teeth and features convulsed with rage, he whirled the instrument of torture round his head and brought it down with all his strength upon the quivering flesh of the lad. Then it was that that heart-rending cry arose through the stillness of the night, scaring the curlews in their seaward flight. The cry was re-echoed by a shout of rage from the people, and by a roar of laughter from the soldiery.

" Let him have it !" cried the officer.

The admonition was unnecessary. Blow after blow fell upon the naked neck, shoulders, and body of the defenceless lad, lacerating the flesh, from which the blood trickled in copious streams ! And the people—what of them ? The women clung to each other, sobbing and moaning. The men clenched their hands and ground their teeth in fury. Big strong men, their hearts bursting, their souls thirsting for vengeance upon the brutal cowards. But they were powerless. Interference meant death to the lad and death to his friends !

Poor Tommy ! After that one wild shriek he bore his agony in silence. His rough, labour-stained hands were clenched until the nails of his fingers cut into his flesh ; he bit his nether lip until it bled. At length his head fell upon his breast ; there was a convulsive writhing of the body, the boy's limbs swayed beneath him, and he became perfectly motionless.

" You have killed him ! " cried one of the soldiers, whose face gave evidence of a kindlier heart than any of his comrades possessed.

As the man spoke, he caught the arm of the executioner and pushed him aside violently.

" The damned young rebel ! " cried the fellow, struggling to free his arm and renew the punishment. The officer stepped forward and looked into Tommy's face.

" Dead as a herring ! " he said, laughing. Turning to the soldier who had whipped the boy, he continued—" Morris, you can hit hard. Put up your whip ; the boy is dead ! "

With a growl of rage the fellow wound the lash of his whip round its handle and stuck it into his belt, then turning to one of his comrades he cried out—" Jemmy, lend me your cropping tools. I'll have his ears ! "

" Ay, ay, my lad," said the soldier addressed, handing the other a large pair of scissors.

They were rusty and blood stained.

Then a rough voice cried—

" We're nae men tae stan' that ! " A big, burly fellow sprang forward, and planting his fist right in the soldier's face, laid him sprawling upon the road.

The man was surrounded in an instant. Clubbing their muskets, the soldiers felled him like an ox, and then, kicking him into a deep ditch that skirted the road, left him bleeding and senseless.

Whether the officer in charge of the soldiers feared further violence or not, it would be difficult to say, but he drew his men hurriedly together, gave the order to march, and the next minute their measured tramp was heard as they started for Newtownards, where they had their headquarters.

A crowd of anxious sympathisers gathered around Tommy Burns. Rough but gentle hands cut the cords which bound him, and carried him into the house. A bed was thrown down upon the kitchen floor, and on this the lad was stretched. In their desire to render him assistance the one for a time impeded the other. But at this juncture the noble spirit which afterwards characterised the beautiful Betsy Gray shone forth. Kneeling by the prostrate lad, she begged the people to stand aside, and then she placed her hand over the region of the boy's heart.

There was a moment or two of breathless silence, of anxious suspense.

" He lives ! " said Betsy.

" Thank God ! " cried several.

" George, help me," cried Betsy.

In an instant her brother and lover were kneeling beside her. She gave her directions quietly, calmly, and apparently without emotion. Such stimulants as were at hand were applied, and ere long the boy opened his eyes. The next moment, with a deep groan, he fainted. Tenderly, unceasingly did that brave girl attend to the sufferer, dressing his swollen and bleeding body, and striving to retain the flickering flame of life. Her efforts were rewarded ! Consciousness returned ; the boy recognised her.

" Are you in pain, Tommy ? " asked Betsy.

" Ay," murmured the lad ; " a feel as if a wuz in a fire."

" Poor boy," she murmured.

Pieces of linen, dipped in cold water, were laid upon the wounds, and afforded temporary relief. Betsy insisted upon having the lad removed to her father's house so that she might nurse him, and he was accordingly carried thither, and placed in a comfortable bed. A doctor was sent for, and everything that skill and careful nursing could accomplish was done for the poor boy who had suffered such brutal torture.

The sturdy young farmer who had rushed to Tommy's rescue was but little the worse of the treatment he received, and was able attend his work a couple of days afterwards.

CHAPTER VII.

" REMEMBER ORR ! "

" Who is she with aspect wild ?
The widow'd mother with her child,
Child now stirring in the womb !
Husband waiting for the tomb ! "—DRENNAN.

FOR a brief space I shift the scene of my story from the shores of County Down to the old town of Carrickfergus, where, just about the date at which my story opens, an incident occurred, full of melancholy interest, and to which historians largely attribute the memorable rising of 1798.

In the month of February, 1796, an Act of Parliament was passed which punished with death the administering of the United Irishman's oath. The awful consequences of this Act were speedily felt. The country swarmed with villains, who recklessly swore away men's lives, earning thereby the blood-money which was lavishly paid from Dublin Castle. Thus it was a crime to administer the oath ; the crime was one easy of proof, and the liberal rewards offered secured to the Government the services of a host of wretches ready and willing to spill the blood of their fellow-men. The English Government intended by this means to stamp out the Society of United Irishmen —a society to which fuller reference will shortly be made in this story. A proclamation was published and posted all through Ireland, stating the provisions of the Act.

The first man tried for the breaking of this law was William Orr, of Ferranshane, in the County of Antrim. He was a farmer, of independent circumstances ; a Presbyterian, and of strict religious principles. He was a man of fine figure and handsome face ; bold, courageous, warm-hearted, and beloved by all who knew him.

Hugh Wheatly, a private soldier in the Fifeshire regiment of Fencibles, swore that in the month of April, 1796, William Orr, in his own house, administered to him the United Irishmen's oath. A comrade of Wheatly's by name Lindsay, corroborated the statement. William Orr was arrested. On the 18th of September, 1797, he was put upon his trial at Carrickfergus. The event created remarkable interest, the court was crowded to excess, and outside hundreds of people eagerly awaited the result. Orr was defended by that able Irish lawyer, Curran, whose speech on the occasion was one of great ability, but that eminent Irish orator failed to save his client. At seven o'clock in the evening the jury retired to consider their verdict and remained in their room till six in the morning. How they spent the night is a matter of history. According to affidavits, sworn afterwards by some of the jurors, numerous bottles of whiskey were passed through the window into the jury-room. The men drank freely, becoming intoxicated, and some of them grew sick from the effects of the liquor. To such men was entrusted the life of a human being ! The jury could not agree to a verdict, but ultimately those in favour of an acquittal were, by intimidation, forced to concur in a finding against Orr.

Amid profound silence the jury entered the court, and the crowd of spectators awaited with breathless interest to hear their finding.

Addressing the jury, the Clerk of the Crown enquired—

" Gentlemen, have you agreed to a verdict ?

There was no reply.

Again the question was put, and, after a long pause, the foreman, an aged man, who appeared to be terribly distressed, answered—

" We leave him in your lordship's mercy ; he is in your lordship's mercy."

The judge remarked that that was not a verdict, and desired the men to return to their room. Ten of them obeyed, the other two stood outside. Again they returned to court, and again the foreman repeated the same words. A third time did the judge send them to their room, and when they next came into court, the foreman still hesitated. One of the jurors—a man named M'Naghten—rebuked the foreman and called upon him to pronounce the prisoner guilty, whereupon he handed in the verdict, accompanied by a recommendation to mercy.

" Prisoner," said the judge, in solemn tones, " have you anything to say why sentence of death should not be passed upon you ? "

" Yes, my lord," was Orr's reply ; and then in a clear voice, that never faltered, he said—

" My friends and fellow-countrymen—In the thirty-first year of my life I have been sentenced to die upon the gallows and this sentence has been in pursuance of a verdict of twelve men, who should have been indifferently and impartially chosen. How far they have been so, I leave that to the country from which they have been chosen to determine ; and how far they have discharged their duty, I leave to their God and to themselves. They have, in pronouncing their verdict, thought proper to recommend me as an object of human mercy. In return, I pray to God to have mercy upon them.

" The law under which I suffer is surely a severe one—may the makers and promoters of it be justified in the integrity of their motives, and the purity of their own lives ! By that law I am stamped a felon but my heart disdains the imputation.

" My comfortable lot and industrious course of life best refute the charge of being an adventurer for plunder ; but if to have loved my country—to have known its wrongs, to have felt the injuries of the persecuted Catholics, and to have united with them and all other religious persuasions in the most orderly and least sanguinary means of procuring redress—if those be felonies, I am a felon, but not otherwise. Had my counsel (for whose honourable exertions I am indebted) prevailed in their motions to have me tried for high treason, rather than under the insurrection law, I should have been entitled to a full defence, and my actions have been better vindicated ; but that was refused, and I must now submit to what has passed.

" To the generous protection of my country I leave a beloved wife, who has been constant and true to me, and whose grief for my fate has already nearly occasioned her death. I have five children living, who have been my delight. May they love their country as I have done, and die for it if needful.

" Lastly, a false and ungenerous publication having appeared in a newspaper, stating certain alleged confessions of guilt on my part, and thus striking at my reputation, which is dearer to me than life, I take this solemn method of contradicting the calumny. I was applied to by the High Sheriff and the Rev. William Bristow, sovereign of Belfast, to make a confession of guilt, and who used entreaties to that effect ; this I peremptorily refused. If I thought myself guilty, I would freely confess it, but, on the contrary, I glory in my innocence.

" I trust that all my virtuous countrymen will bear me in their kind remembrance, and continue true and faithful to each other as I have been to all of them. With this last wish of my heart—nothing doubting of the success of that cause for which I suffer, and hoping for God's merciful forgiveness of such offences as my frail nature may have at any time betrayed me into—I die in peace and charity with all mankind."

CHAPTER VIII.

THE FIRST VICTIM.

" They led him forth from his prison cell !
They swung him high on the gallows tree !
And the people wept as the brave man died—
Died for his faith and counterie. "—OLD BALLAD.

SENTENCE of death was passed upon William Orr. The judge wept freely ; the people sobbed, but Orr stood unmoved. At the close of Judge Yelverton's sentence Orr was removed to prison, there to await the final scene.

The 7th of October was fixed for the execution, and in the interval various representations, favourable and adverse to Orr, were forwarded to the Executive. One of these was of so strong a nature that it is impossible to conceive why it could have been overlooked by the Government. Affidavits were sworn by some of the jurors to the effect that they had been driven by threats to concur in the verdict of guilty, and it was also clearly proven that Wheatly, the informer, was a profligate scoundrel, upon whose oath even a dog should not have been hung. As a result of the efforts made by his friends, Orr was respited till the 10th of October, and again till the 14th. Memorials signed by the most influential men in the County of Antrim were sent to the Lord Lieutenant, praying for a pardon, nay, *demanding* the pardon as an act either of mercy, justice, or policy. But all in vain !

Saturday morning the 14th of October, 1797, dawned clear and bright upon the old town of Carrickfergus. It dawned upon many an eye red with weeping, on many an untouched pillow, for the news had gone forth that William Orr, the idol of the people, was to die. Blinds were drawn, shops were closed, everywhere signs of sorrow and mourning were visible.

At the prescribed hour Orr emerged from his prison cell. His imprisonment and the days and nights of mental agony and suspense which he must have endured had robbed his cheeks of their glow of health ; but he stood before the minions of the law erect in all his manly beauty, his handsome face wearing a look of calm resignation, and his eye quailing not in presence of his grim surroundings.

It was intimated to the unfortunate man that a post chaise had been provided to drive to the place of execution, but he declined to use it, fearing that he might be separated from his friends and that soldiers might be his companions. He expressed the wish to have the company of the Rev. Mr. Stavley and the Rev. Mr. Hill upon his journey to the scaffold, and these gentlemen were permitted to sit with him in the carriage. The authorities evidently feared an attempt at rescue. There was a strong military guard, composed of horse, foot, and artillery, detached from different regiments in Belfast and Carrickfergus. At the place of execution the infantry were drawn up in the form of a triangle round the gallows ; on the outside of the infantry the cavalry continued to move, while at some distance two cannons were planted, commanding the Carrickfergus and Belfast roads.

But these precautions were unnecessary. The people shunned the sight of this unpardonable butchery, and, shutting themselves up in their houses, prayed for the painless death and eternal happiness of the martyr Orr.

When the gallows had been reached, Orr shook hands with his friends, and with an heroic attempt at cheerfulness which he could not have felt, told them to bear up bravely. With a firm step he mounted the fatal ladder, and drawing up his fine manly figure to its full height, looked unflinchingly upon the dangling rope and the bristling arms of the soldiery. The hangman stealthily advanced and slipped the noose round the neck of the condemned man. As he did so an indignant flush spread over Orr's features, and in a loud voice he exclaimed—

" I am no traitor ! I am persecuted for my country. I die in the true faith of a Presbyterian."

The next moment the ladder was kicked away, and the soul of the first victim stood before its God !

Such was the fate of William Orr, one of the noblest men who ever breathed, and thus he died by the hand of a wicked and blood-stained Government. The seeds of revolt which had taken root in the hearts of the people were nourished by his blood, his name was stamped upon their pikes, and in many a bloody encounter which followed upon the fields of Antrim and Down, the rallying word of the Irish patriots was—

" REMEMBER ORR ! "

The fury of the people was boundless. Not in Ireland alone was the sad and cruel fate of Orr mourned for, but even in the capital of England, where, at a public dinner, Mr. Fox gave the memory of the martyr, and another speaker proposed as a sentiment—" May the Irish Cabinet soon take the place of William Orr ! "

CHAPTER IX.

MAT M'CLENAGHAN'S CONSCIENCE.

" My heart is sair, ay, unco sair ;
Oh, losh ! my stamach's racked wi' pain ;
Oh, gin a wuz but sober, lass,
A niver wad get fu' again ! "—ROBIN.

IT would be impossible to describe the rage and mortification of Mat M'Clenaghan, the honest blacksmith, when, on the morning after the christening, he awoke and was informed by his wife, Bel, of the occurrences of the preceding night. For a while he seemed to doubt his wife's sincerity and to regard the matter as a joke, and indeed it was not until he went over to Mr. Hans Gray's and saw Tommy Burns lying in bed, moaning piteously, that he could be brought to realise the true state of affairs.

The sight was more than Mat's kindly nature could bear. He turned away with a moistened eye, and without uttering a word, retraced his steps homeward. He found a kindly neighbour, the wife of a farmer named John Moore, sitting with his wife and doing her best to soothe the poor woman's troubled mind.

Mat, dear, this is a sayrious business," said Mrs. Moore, as Mat entered.

" Ay, wuman, that it is ! " said Mat, " but a doot we hae only seen the beginnin' o' it."

" Wuzn't it Guid's mercy that ye had nae pikes lyin' aboot ? " went on Mrs. Moore.

" A'm no sae saft as a' that," replied Mat ; " but there's yin thing, Mistress Moore, as lang as a'm a leevin' man a'll niver get sae beastly drunk as a wuz last night."

Mat's wife said nothing, but sat rocking her cradle and moaning pitifully.

" Jest tae think o't ! " exclaimed Mat, his temper rising, " my helpless waen cloddit aboot like a cat an' that puir crayter Tammy akwelly cut in pieces, an' a' through me bein' drunk. Be haivens if a had been astir they wudnae a had it a' their ain wae. A wush sumbudy had drappit a pun' o' gun-pooder in the fire an' blawed the bluidy rid-coats tae smithereens ! "

" A wunner what things ir cummin till," murmured Mrs. Moore. As she spoke she passed her hand backwards and forwards over the surface of a teapot which lay upon her lap. She had lent it to Mrs. M'Clenaghan for the christening and had now called to take it back.

" Ye may weel say that," cried Mat ; " ye may weel wunner what things ir cummin tae. Why, wuman, luk here—"

As Mat spoke he stepped forward and took the teapot from Mrs. Moore's lap, and held it up to view. On one side were the words,

" Liberty and Property," on the other, " Peace to America."

" Luk here ! " continued Mat " afore lang it'll be a hangin' metter to let the like o' that be seen aboot a buddy's hoose. Nice times indeed tae leev in ! "

Mat in his cooler moments would not have made such a statement, and would have laughed had he heard any other person make use of similar language. And yet he spoke truly prophetically. So stringent were the measures adopted by the Government that it was considered treasonable to have possession of any articles bearing such mottoes. That very teapot, which did service in Mat M'Clenaghan's house in the month of October, 1797, was afterwards buried in the owner's garden for safety, and at this day is in the possession of Mr. George Moore, postmaster, Ballygrainey, Six-Road-Ends, who is the great-grandson of its original owner.

Mat went to his work, and left the two women together. The door of his smiddy was open, and his tools lay scattered about where they had been tossed by the soldiers. He muttered fierce imprecations as he gathered them together, and then lit his forge fire. He was in no mood for work, but he felt he must do something to drive away the thoughts which had taken possession of him. And here an incident occurred which is talked of in the neighbourhood even to the present day.

As Mat puffed away with his bellows and watched the red flame shooting upwards, two farmers from the Cottown entered, each bringing the " sock " of a plough to be repaired. Both men were in a hurry, and each urged Mat to do his job first in order. Mat lifted both socks and thrust them into the fire. Like a man in a dream he blew his bellows until the irons were red hot, then removing them to the anvil, he seized his hammer, and, in a fit of utter abstraction, welded the two socks completely together, while the farmers looked on in silent amazement.

" There ! " he exclaimed, as he flung his hammer into a corner, " awa oot o' this an' gie me peace ! "

The men saw how matters stood and left Mat to his own thoughts. He was an odd creature, Mat ; hot-headed, kind-hearted, and ready-witted. Many of his sayings are still current. One night as he was busily engaged hammering out a pike upon his anvil, a confidential friend remarked to him—

" Mat, after all it's dangerous work, and perhaps sinful this making of pikes."

Mat paused in his work, and, as he held up the pike-head in his left hand and the hammer in his right, he laughingly retorted—

" Damn it, man, shair iverything's beautiful in its saison ! "

The saying got abroad and was in common use long after Mat and his smiddy had disappeared. When a farmer came home from Newton market or fair and was being rebuked by his wife for having partaken of too many " half ones," he would quote from Mat's philosophy, and say—

" Agh, haud yer tongue, wuman, shair iverything's nice in its saison ! "

That afternoon Mat had a visit from George Gray—Betsy's brother—and the two had a long and earnest consultation. George intimated to Mat that there would be a " meeting " that night in his house, that Willie Boal had at last consented to join the popular cause, and that he would that night be initiated into the order of the United Irishmen.

" A'll be there ! " said Mat, as a grim smile illuminated his features. " A wuz niver sae earnest in the wark as a feel mysel' noo ! " I want my readers to go also, that they may have a peep at a lodge of United Irishmen, and learn something of their mission and of their doings. Turn your steps with me, kind reader, towards the homestead of our brave heroine, Betsy Gray, of Granshaw.

CHAPTER X.

THE UNITED IRISHMEN.

" They rose in dark and evil days
To right their native land ;
They kindled here a living blaze
That nothing shall withstand. "

AMONGST my readers there are doubtless very many who know but little of the history of the society or organisation called United Irishmen. To give details of the numerous and varied organisations which, up till the date of my story, had existed in Ireland would certainly weary my readers. These can be found in the pages of Irish history. A word, however, respecting the United Irishmen is here absolutely necessary.

In the month of March, 1791, there assembled in a public house in Sugar-house Entry, Belfast—still in existence—a few young and bold spirits, chiefly Presbyterians, to whom had occurred the idea of uniting Irishmen of all creeds and parties in one common bond, for the purpose of obtaining, or seeking to obtain, a more equitable adjustment of constitutional laws. They believed that the great defect in all previous movements for a redress of political grievances was the sectarian bigotry which excluded the Catholics from any participation in the blessings of reform. They held that the hope of obtaining a full representation of the people in Parliament, whilst two thirds of them were to be excluded from any share in it, was absurd. Some of those who met that day were destined to live in history. The company included Neilson, M'Cracken, Simms, Sinclaire, M'Clean, M'Cabe, Russell, Orr, Hassett and M'Tiernan. Neilson, in a speech which he delivered upon the occassion, said—" our efforts for reform have hitherto been ineffectual, and they deserve to be so, for they have been selfish and unjust, as not including the rights of the Catholics in the claims we put forward for ourselves."

Those men at once set about the formation of a society which should be neither sectarian nor exclusive, but whose objects should be the amelioration of the whole people of Ireland. A general meeting was held in Belfast in the month of October, 1791, and the list of members enrolled thereat contained the names of men of the highest standing among the gentry, merchants and traders. The society grew rapidly. Discontent had been filling the minds of the people ; the persecuting spirit displayed by Government authorities and the despotism of the military were calculated to create and foster this discontent.

Certain concessions were made to the Catholics in 1793, but these were dissipated by the policy of coercion resumed in 1794, and which increased in vigour until the rebellion exploded in 1798. The Convention Act virtually took away the right of public meeting, and it was the subsequent operation of this Act against the meetings of the United Irishmen that changed their tactics and rendered secret proceedings necessary. They had given offence to Government by the boldness of their views and by the change which they had effected upon the public mind relative to Catholic claims. On the 4th May, 1794, a meeting of United Irishmen in Dublin was attacked by the police, the members dispersed, and their papers seized. From this period different plans were adopted. The popular name—United Irishmen—was retained, but the test was amended, as was also the method of organisation. Provincial committees, county committees and baronial committees were formed, while an oath of secrecy was added. Each society consisted of twelve members, who chose a secretary and treasurer. The secretary was known as sergeant or corporal ; the delegate of five societies to a lower baronial was called captain, having sixty men under his command; the delegate of ten lower baronials to the upper or district committee was usually the colonel, and thus a battalion was composed of six hundred. The colonels of each county sent in the names of three persons to the executive, one of whom was appointed by the executive to be adjutant-general of the county, and his duty was to receive and communicate all military orders from the executive.

Thus did the military organisation grow out of the civil system and the Government were well informed of this from April 14th, 1797.

I have already informed my readers that, in the month of February, 1796, an Act of Parliament was passed which punished with death the administering of the United Irishmen's oath. That year was an eventful one. The Government paid informers generally, and the country swarmed with ruffians ready to betray their nearest and dearest friends. In one year the sum of £38,419 8s. was thus paid away. Government spies were in every town and village ; outrages of the most terrible kind were perpetrated. Neilson, Russell, and M'Cracken—three of the leading spirits who at the meeting in Sugarhouse Entry, Belfast, promulgated the objects of the society—were now marked men, and an incident occurred in connection with them which is worthy of mention, standing out, as it does, in noble contrast with the treachery of many worthless scoundrels of the time. A poor weaver, who lived in Brown Square, was an intelligent member of the United Irishmen, and was known to be thoroughly acquainted with their movements. One evening he was called upon by an attorney who, after some conversation, offered him £500 if he would inform upon Neilson, Russell and M'Cracken. To the man's eternal honour be it told that he indignantly refused the bribe, and going straight to the houses of the three gentlemen he warned them of their danger.

Of a different stamp was Nick Maginn, of Saintfield. Nick was a poor creature holding a few acres of ground. He joined the United Irishmen, attained (according to his own statement) the rank of colonel, and from the 14th of April, 1797, he kept the Government fully informed of the operations of the United Irishmen in and about Saintfield. He went to every meeting held in his district, and immediately afterwards communicated to the Rev. John Cleland all that passed. He also supplied lists of arms and ammunition, names of members and other information. Wealth he certainly acquired, for Government rewarded him liberally. In a published list of the sums paid to informers the following two items appear :—

" August 16, 1798,	N. Maginn,	£700	0	0	
„ 17, „	do.	56	17	6."	

CHAPTER XI.

TAKING THE OATH.

" With hopeful hearts we pledge once more
Our gentle sister guests !
We drew our love of Gaelic lore
From Irish mothers' breasts.
Then, comrades, let us proudly toast
These priceless Celtic pearls—
Real shamrock buds, the exile's boast,
Green Erin's Patriot Girls ! "

PRIOR to the year 1797, Mr. Hans Gray, Betsy Gray's father, removed from the house where he had lived, and in which Betsy had been born. His farm, then a large one, he divided with a brother, who took up his abode in Betsy's birthplace, while Mr.

Hans Gray and his family—George and Betsy—went to a house which stood upon the ground at present occupied by the office-houses of Mr. James Knox, of Granshaw.

It was in this house that the " meeting " spoken of by George Gray to our friend, Mat M'Clenaghan, was to be held.

The night was dark and rainy, but neither rain nor darkness prevented the twelve members who constituted one of the Granshaw societies from being punctually at their posts. It is of course a well-known fact that many females were admitted to the meetings, and there were two present on this occasion. These were Betsy Gray and Eliza Bryson, whose father, a respectable farmer living at the Cottown, had risen to the rank of colonel.

The usual meetings of the United Irishmen were often of a most jovial description. Tea and its accompaniments were served, followed, generally, by punch. The qualifications of candidates were discussed ; songs were sung ; stories told ; speeches delivered.

But to-night a shade of gloom was upon every countenance, and the silence was almost painful. In the parlour, tea had been laid, and the wants of the guests were attended to by Miss Gray and Miss Bryson ; while Mr. Hans Gray did his best to keep up the fitful and flagging conversation. When the tea things had been removed, Colonel Bryson suggested a song, and this suggestion was warmly supported. There were frequent calls for Mat M'Clenaghan, but that worthy was in bad form.

" Agh, boys, A'm railly no fit fur singin' the nicht," he remonstrated several times, but no denial would be taken.

" Betsy ! " cried Mr. Gray.

" Yes, father."

" Bring some hot water and glasses, with something else that you know where to find."

In a few minutes glasses of steaming punch were passed round, and Mat, who had very nearly resolved upon being a teetotaller, drained his tumbler with a sigh of relief.

" Now, Mat ! " said the colonel.

Mat required no pressing. He cleared his throat, and rattled off a song which had already acquired great popularity in Ireland. For the benefit of my readers I here produce it:—

THE SHAN VAN VACHT

OH ! the French are on the sea,
Says the Shan Van Vacht ;
The French are on the sea,
Says the Shan Van Vacht ;
Oh ! the French are in the Bay,
They'll be here without delay,
And tyrants will decay,
Says the Shan Van Vacht.

CHORUS.

Oh ! the French are in the Bay,
They'll be here by break of day,
And tyrants will decay,
Says the Shan Van Vacht.

And where will they have their camp ?
Says the Shan Van Vacht;
Where will they have their camp ?
Says the Shan Van Vacht ;
On the Curragh of Kildare,
The boys they will be there
With their pikes in good repair,
Says the Shan Van Vacht.

To the Curragh of Kildare
The boys they will repair,
And Lord Edward will be there,
Says the Shan Van Vacht.

Then what will the Yeomen do ?
Says the Shan Van Vacht ;
What WILL the Yeomen do ?
Says the Shan Van Vacht ;
What SHOULD the Yeomen do
But throw off the red and blue,
And swear that they'll be true
To the Shan Van Vacht.

What SHOULD the Yeomen do
But throw off the red and blue,
And swear that they'll be true
To the Shan Van Vacht.

And what colour will they wear ?
        Says the Shan Van Vacht;
What colour will they wear ?
        Says the Shan Van Vacht;
What colour should be seen
Where our fathers' homes have been,
But their own immortal green ?
        Says the Shan Van Vacht.

What colour should be seen
Where our fathers' homes have been,
But their own immortal green ?
        Says the Shan Van Vacht.

And will Ireland then be free ?
        Says the Shan Van Vacht;
Will Ireland then be free ?
        Says the Shan Van Yacht;
Yes ! Ireland shall be free,
From the centre to the sea ;
Then hurrah for Liberty !
        Says the Shan Van Vacht.

Yes ! Ireland shall be free,
From the centre to the sea ;
Then hurrah for Liberty !
        Says the Shan Van Vacht.

Hearty plaudits followed Mat's song, and then the company settled down to business. At a signal from Mr. Gray, who occupied an armchair at the head of the table, there was silence for a moment or two, and he then said:—

" I am pleased to inform you that our good friend, Mr. William Boal, has resolved to be one of us. For reasons best known to himself, he has until now held aloof from our brotherhood, though he did not disapprove of our objects. Colonel Bryson, will you, with George and John Moore, accompany Willie Boal and myself to the other room ? "

Mr. Gray rose and stepped into a bedroom opening off the parlour, and the persons mentioned followed him.

Addressing Willie Boal, he said—

" Do you come here to join the Society of United Irishmen of your own free will and accord ? "

" I do," replied Boal.

" Then take this pamphlet," continued Mr. Gray, handing Boal a paper consisting of eight pages of printed matter. " This contains the declaration which you will now be required to take, also the rules of our society and other matters. Are you now prepared to take the oath ?"

" I am" said Willie, as he took the Bible extended to him by Mr. Gray.

" Then say after me."

The oath, which was as follows, was then administered ; Boal, according to instructions, holding the Bible and the Constitution upon his right breast :—

" In the awful presence of God, I, William Boal, do voluntarily declare that I will persevere in endeavouring to form a brotherhood of affection among Irishmen of every religious persuasion ; and that I will also persevere in my endeavours to obtain an equal, full, and adequate representation of all the people of Ireland. I do further declare that neither hopes, fears, rewards nor punishments shall ever induce me, directly or indirectly, to inform on, or give evidence against, any member or members of this or similar societies, for any act or expression of theirs done or made, collectively or individually in or out of this society, in pursuance of the spirit of this obligation. "

The oath taken, Mr. Gray proceeded to instruct the new member.

" We have a mode of recognising members of the brotherhood," said Gray : " for instance, if a person addressing you repeats the first letter of the word ' United ' thus—' I know U,' you are to reply, ' I know N.' Your interrogator will then say, ' I know I,' and so you both proceed until the word ' United ' has been spelled. There are also several questions and answers in use, for instance—

Q.—' Are you straight ? '

A.—' I am.'

Q.—' How straight ? '

A.—' As straight as a rush.'

Q.—' Go on then ? '

A.—' In truth, in trust, in unity, and liberty.'

Q.—' What have you got in your hand ? '

A.—' A green bough.'

Q.—' Where did it first grow ? '

A.—' In America.'

Q.—' Where did it bud ? '

A.—' In France.'

Q.—' Where are you going to plant it ? '

A.—' In the crown of Great Britain.' "

At the close of the instructions, Boal was warmly congratulated by the members, the books and papers were put away in a safe place, the parlour door was unlocked, and festivities were resumed.

Little did these people dream of the terrible ordeals through which they would shortly have to pass. And now, after this necessary digression, let me proceed with the exciting events which reached their awful climax on the 13th of June, 1798.

CHAPTER XII.

THE DRUMAWHEY INFORMER.

" The noble Warwick was betrayed
By cold and cruel villain ;
A mother's curse shall ever cling
To the informer, Dillon ! "—OLD BALLAD.

JAMES DILLON bequeathed to his descendants—if such there be—the heritage of infamy. Nearly a century has passed since the commission of his crime, but many centuries shall elapse ere his name shall be mentioned in County Down save as that of a ruffian and a scoundrel.

Dillon kept a common public house in the townland of Drumawhey, near Newtownards. He also kept a school there. From what has already been said of him in a previous chapter, the reader will have seen that he was far from being a favourite with the people of his district, and that at least one man suspected him of being an informer. Mat M'Clenaghan suspected him, and subsequent events proved that Mat was correct in his suspicions.

At the date of my story there resided in Drumawhey a Mrs. Warwick—a widow who held a farm of land, working it as best she could. She was a woman universally respected, and the horse and plough of many a well-to-do farmer in the country side was at her service whenever required. Mrs. Warwick had an only son—William—and he was the pride of her heart, the hope of her declining years. From an early age the lad had displayed abilities of a high order. He was of a religious turn of mind, and his father destined him for the pulpit—a choice of profession which in every way pleased young William.

At the time of the occurrences which have just been related William Warwick had finished, and that, too, with high reputation, his collegiate course. He was connected with the Belfast Presbytery and as a probationer awaited an appointment to a pastoral charge. He was a young man of much promise, learning and eloquence. Polished in his manners, imposing in his appearance, with the carriage of the soldier and the ardour of the patriot, he was the welcome visitor of everyone in the neighbourhood. This very popularity of the handsome young probationer, and his scholarly ability, seemed to cast Dillon, the country schoolmaster, completely in the shade. Dillon secretly swore that he would be revenged, and he kept his word.

One cold, dark night, not long after the swearing in of Willie Boal as a United Irishman, a number of farmers were seated round a fire in a little room in Dillon's public house. They had been drinking freely, and, feeling no suspicion of danger, were discussing openly the probability of an early rising.

" A hae a bit o' writin' in my pokit," said one of them—Sam Donaldson by name—" that wud mebbe gie ye a bit o' infurmaishin if ye only seen it."

" Shew it tae us, Sam ! " cried the others, eagerly.

But Sam laughed, and buttoning up his coat, tapped the breast of it. Then with a knowing wink, he said—

" A micht be an adjutant-general sum day, boys ; a'm in trainin' fur it onywae, an' a wud be gie an' saft if a wud shew ye the furst dispatch that wuz gien me tae carry ! "

" Richt, Sam ! Richt, my boy ! " was the cry of several, but a few there were who wanted to see the document, the very mention of which had aroused so much interest.

" Damn the paper he haes, nae mauir nor a hae !" growled a burly, big-headed fellow, and as he made the assertion he brought down his ponderous fist upon the table with a thump that upset half-a-dozen tumblers.

This put Sam upon his mettle, and doubtless it was so intended. He jumped to his feet, unbuttoned his coat, and drawing out a document, unfolded it and held it up.

" Hand the cannel here, yin o' ye ! " he shouted.

There was a scramble for who should do so, and the big-headed fellow was the first to get a look at the paper.

" Noo, dinnae read it ! " shouted Sam ; " jist luk wha's name's at it."

The man did so, and sat down.

" A beg yer pardin, Sam," he said. " A'm shair it's a' richt by the name a see at the fut o' it."

" So ye may," retorted Sam, an' mair betoken it's a' in the handwritin' o' his reverince, Mister Warwick ! "

" Weel, weel," said the big fellow, " a'll order drinks fur a' roon on the heid o't."

So saying he rose from the table to repair to the bar. As he did so, a woman darted away from the outer side of the door, and stole noiselessly into another room.

It was Dillon's wife ! She had stood with her eye at the keyhole, and seen and heard all !

The liquor was served, and Dillon, as he returned to the bar, was accosted by his wife, in a whisper, from the apartment to which she had retreated.

" Jamey ! Come here."

He was at her side in a moment. She told him what she had heard ; what she had seen.

When Dillon returned to the bar his face bore a look of unmistakeable satisfaction. With both hands plunged deep in his trousers' pockets, he paced up and down the damp earthen floor, buried in thought. His mind seemed busily engaged in the solution of a problem, and at length he appeared to have arrived at that solution.

His customers had grown noisy. One of the party was singing a song, and the others joined in the chorus. It was a ditty of the day. At its conclusion, they rose to depart. As they passed through the bar, some of them stopped to light their pipes. Sam Donaldson was one of these, and as he buttoned up his coat, and said good-night, Dillon with a wink and an inclination of his head, signified that he wished him to remain after the others had left. Sam understood the hint, and acted upon it. Turning to his companions he said—

" Boys, a'm no gaun hame yit awhile. A hae sum bizziness tae dae wi' Mister Dillon."

" A' richt, Sam ; guid nicht, guid nicht," chorused the others, and off they went, leaving Sam and the landlord together.

" Come and have a quiet glass of punch," said Dillon ; " I want to speak to you."

"A wull dae that," replied Sam, readily. He had already overstepped the boundary line of moderation, and another glass, in his opinion, would do him no harm.

Dillon brewed two tumblers of punch. He used no measure on this occasion, and he helped Sam with an unsparing hand. Whiskey was cheap in those days, but the landlord expected a good turn for his hospitality.

" Now, Sam, try that," he said, drawing a small table to the fire and placing the steaming liquor close to his guest's elbow. Then he sat down beside him.

" Yer helth an' lang life tae ye ! " said Sam, and he took a deep draught of the potent spirit.

" Yours ! " said Dillon, sipping the punch slowly, and watching his companion closely to note how far he was from the borders of intoxication. He was not far !

" Tell me, Sam," said Dillon, " haven't you a fancy for that farm of Gunion's that marshes your land ? "

" Man, a hae that," cried Sam, brightening up

" There's a chance of your getting it," said Dillon.

It was then that men were made to hanker after their neighbour's farm ; bidding high for it at a sale, getting it by means often foul. And so landlords profited by the cupidity of tenants, pocketed the big rents, and laughed. The tenants were often to blame.

Sam considered for a few moments, then, looking up, said mysteriously—

" *Is it at the deveesion o' the land a'll get it ?* "

Dillon laughed.

" No, Sam ; there won't be any division such as you dream of, my boy."

" A'm no sae shair o' that! " said Sam ; " they'll be drawin' cuts fur it afore lang, and fur ocht ye ken Mountstewart or Rosemount micht be cut up."

Unobserved, Dillon replenished Sam's glass, and that worthy drained it.

" I meant to tell you," went on Dillon, " that Gunion is so far in arrears with his rent that he must give up. If you like I'll mention your name to the landlord as his successor."

Sam was drunk. He glared at Dillon stupidly, and then he spread his arms upon the table, laid his head upon them, and the next minute was sound asleep.

Dillon waited, watching Sam as a cat would a mouse.

" Mary ! " he whispered.

Mary was his wife, and she had been hovering near. In an instant she was at his side.

" Stand between us and the window," whispered Dillon.

The woman understood him, and took up her position as directed.

Dillon caught Sam by the collar and shook him. As he did so, he jerked out the buttons of the man's coat.

" Wake up Sam ! " he said.

But the fellow was oblivous to everything,

" *Which pocket ?* " whispered Dillon.

The woman pointed to it with her finger.

In another moment a folded sheet of paper, foolscap size, had passed from Sam's pocket to that of Dillon.

The cowardly theft had not been committed a moment too soon. The door opened and one of Sam's former companions entered.

" Is Sam awa ? " he asked.

" No," said Dillon, rising, " here he is, snoring like a hog."

The man stepped up to the fire and attempted to rouse the sleeper, but in vain.

" I wish you would take him away," said Dillon ; " I want to close up."

The man went to the door and whistled. He was soon joined by a neighbour, and the two undertook to have Sam left safely home.

" Take a drink of something before you go," said Dillon.

It was seldom he stood a drink, and the men were not in the humour to decline his hospitality. His hand was not so steady as usual in filling the glasses, but his wife alone noted that fact.

The men drank their liquor, and then left, half dragging, half carrying their inebriated companion.

Dillon followed them to the door, looking around to see if all was clear, closed the swing shutter, went inside again and barred the door.

Advancing hurriedly to the light, he drew out the document and glanced carefully over its contents. As he did so, a grim smile overspread his features. Folding it up again he placed it in his pocket.

His wife peering into his face, enquired—

" Weel ? "

" It's worth five hundred pounds if it's worth a penny ! " said Dillon excitedly. " To-morrow morning I'll start for Newton and place this before the authorities. Before twenty-four hours we'll have lively scenes in Drumawhey."

CHAPTER XIII.

WILLIAM WARWICK.

" And there are creatures, in the form of men,
Who crawl, as reptiles crawl, upon the earth,
They breathe but poison. 'Tis beyond our ken
If ought save Hell e'er smiled upon their birth." —LYTTLE.

IT was late that night before Dillon went to bed. It was later still before he slept. Again and again did he peruse the paper writing which had come into his hands, and, as he did so, he gloated savagely over the fate which he knew would now to a certainty overtake Warwick. The document was partly in cipher and partly in ordinary writing. It was an outline of preparations to be made in view of a call to arms, and the name attached to it was that of one of the leading members of the United Irishmen Organisation. Warwick was not responsible for the framing of this document. He had merely, by request, made a copy of it for Colonel Bryson. This was the only political offence ever laid to Warwick's charge, yet it was one which in those days was quite sufficient to bring a man before a military court-martial, and from thence to the gallows. Yet was he, in reality, as innocent of political crime as the child unborn.

Dillon spent a restless night. The hope of gain, the fear of detection as an informer, filled his mind alternately, and drove sleep from his eyes. Towards the morning he dropped into a fitful slumber, which gradually deepened into a heavy sleep, and when at last he awoke with a sudden start, it was to hear the wheezy old eight-day clock which stood in the bedroom striking the hour of nine.

He sprang out of bed with an oath upon his lips. Nine o'clock ! Why, he meant to have been at Newton and back before that hour. In a mood the reverse of pleasant he put on his clothes. After all, what did it matter ? He could go after school hours and when darkness had set in. And so he set himself to the monotonous routine of his daily calling.

And what of his intended victim, Warwick ? The unsuspecting youth rose with a clear brain and a light heart, little dreaming of the cloud which was gathering over his head. On entering the little room which had been set apart as his study, he found, as usual, a cheery turf fire burning brightly in the old-fashioned grate, and breakfast laid upon a little round table covered with a snow white cloth.

Mother and son breakfasted together, and, as the meal proceeded, Warwick told his mother of his intended movements for the day. He had numerous letters to write, sundry calls to make in the neighbourhood, and in the evening he was to attend a select party to be given by Betsy Gray—the annual celebration of her mother's marriage day.

" Then you'll be late, William," said Mrs. Warwick, as she helped on her son's overcoat.

" Yes, mother ; but don't be uneasy, and don't be sitting up for me, mind that."

The widowed mother smiled sadly.

" I'm always uneasy when you are out late," she said ; " these are such troublesome times."

" Nonsense, mother," laughed Warwick, as he kissed her pale cheek, " what harm can befall me ?"

" God keep you under the shelter of His wings, William," was the fervent response.

" And He will do so," said Warwick earnestly. " They who put their trust in Him shall not be disappointed."

The next moment he was gone.

His mother had followed him to the door, and she stood there looking after him with eyes dimmed by tears until he was out of sight. Then she closed the door, and, with a heavy sigh, set about her household duties.

Had the mother's heart a foreboding of what was to happen to her darling boy ?

* * * * * * * * * * *

How cheery did Betsy Gray's parlour look that evening at five o'clock ! The curtains were drawn, the fire bright, the brass kettle singing merrily upon the hob. The candles were lit, the table laid, and Betsy herself, decked out in a charming costume, flitted about, light as a fairy, imparting to the general arrangements a finishing touch.

" What keeps Mary I wonder," she murmured, half aloud, " she promised to be here soon after dinner."

The very next moment the room door opened, there was a ripple of laughter, a rustling of silk, and she of whom Betsy had been speaking caught her in her arms and kissed her.

For certain obvious reasons the real names of several personages who figure prominently in this story are not given. No apology is needed for this, and the reader's own good taste and judgment will approve of the writer's desire not to draw aside too far the veil which has fallen upon incidents connected with the history of many who still reside in districts where these pages are certain to be read.

Mary Stewart (so she shall be called) was one of Betsy Gray's most intimate acquaintances. She was young, well educated, warm-hearted, affectionate, and of prepossessing appearance. She was the affianced of William Warwick, whom she first met under Betsy's roof, and many a pleasant evening had they spent there.

" Mary, darling, what kept you ? " cried Betsy, as she caught the pretty face between her hands and looked into the laughing pair of eyes before whose glances Warwick had surrendered.

" I could not come sooner, indeed, dear," replied Mary. " After all, I am first upon the scene. Who will be here, Betsy ? "

She laid aside her bonnet and shawl as she spoke, and took the armchair which Betsy had placed for her.

" Who will be here, Mary ? " said Betsy, as she sat down beside her companion on a low footstool. " Only a few, my dear. Colonel Bryson and Eliza, my father and George, and—"

" And —— " said Mary laughing and patting Betsy's rosy cheek. " I think I can guess—Willie Boal, isn't it ? "

" Well, yes ; and another Willie, too," said Betsy. " Ah, there he is ; I hear his voice," and she started up to meet the new comer in the kitchen.

Mary had heard the voice also ; the rich musical tones of her lover, and a tell-tale blush suffused her lovely cheeks.

There was a cordial handshaking, and then Betsy, with true womanly feeling, left the lovers by themselves as long as it was possible for her to do so under the circumstances. Warwick had much to tell Mary. He had heard from his Presbytery, or from the Clerk of it, of an expected call from a flourishing congregation.

" If I succeed, Mary," he murmured, " I shall be in a position to claim the fulfilment of your promise, and then—— "

" I shall be ready," she whispered.

" My darling," said Warwick, " my own darling ! Life shall be too short to tell you how much I love you ! "

Poor Warwick !

* * * * * * * * * * *

Half an hour later a pleasant party surrounded Betsy's table. It was thus that for years she had celebrated the anniversary of her mother's marriage. There was nothing that was melancholy about these celebrations. Mrs. Gray, the wife and mother, was spoken of as an absent friend ; as a loved one at a distance, whose companionship would some day be restored to them.

The meal had been over some time ; the occupants of the parlour were seated around the fire discussing various topics, when a tap was heard at the room door.

It was the servant girl who announced that Sam Donaldson wished to speak to Mr. Bryson.

" Shew him in," said George Gray.

The man entered, and looked around him in a half dazed manner, as though blinded by the light.

" Sit down, Sam," said George, rising and offering a chair.

" Na, thank ye, Mester George, all no be sittin'," said Sam, casting down his eyes, and twirling his hat between his hands.

" Do you want to speak to me, Sam ? " asked Colonel Bryson.

" Yis, sir, if ye pleese ; mebbe ye wud be sae kin' as tae step ootside fur a minit."

" Certainly," replied the Colonel, rising and following Sam, who led the way through the kitchen and out into the open air.

For fully ten minutes the two men were earnestly engaged in conversation. At the end of that time they returned to the parlour. The look of alarm which was on the colonel's face had the effect of bringing George Gray and his father to their feet instantly.

" What is the matter ? " asked George hurriedly.

" Something has occurred which may prove to be a very serious misfortune to one or more of us," replied the colonel, in a voice rendered tremulous by excitement.

" Let us hear it," cried several.

" Better not to alarm the ladies ; it might be well that they should retire," suggested Warwick.

" Oh, no, papa ; that would only make us worse ; do let us hear it," pleaded Eliza Bryson.

" Yes, do," urged Betsy, while Mary, now pale as death, clung tremblingly to Warwick's arm.

" Be it so," said the colonel. Then, looking at Warwick, he continued—

" Sam has lost that document with which you entrusted him yesterday."

" Lost it ! " gasped Warwick.

The men exchanged glances ; they knew in a moment what the announcement meant, but they could not suppose what dreadful consequences might ensue.

" Where did you lose it, Sam ? " asked George Gray sharply.

"A dinnae ken, indeed, indeed, sur," said Sam, who was dreadfully cut up.

" He was drunk while it was in his possession," said the colonel.

" Where ? " asked Warwick.

" In Dillon's public house."

Here Sam was appealed to by George Gray.

" Come, Sam," he said, " pull yourself together like a man. Clear your head and think. This may be a bad affair for all of us. When had you this document—when did you last see it ? "

" A had it in Dillon's ; a'm shair o' that, fur a min' showin' it tae sum o' the boys. Whun we wur gaen awa, Dillon signed at me fur tae wait ahint the rest. A did that, an' he gien me a wheen o' drinks. A min' naethin mair till a waukened up this mornin', an' whun a lukit my pokit the paper wuz awa. "

" Dillon stole it, by God ! " cried the colonel.

" How could he know of its existence ? " asked George.

" It may have fallen from Sam's pocket. Sam, Sam, this is a bad business," said Betsy.

Sam was wringing his hands in agony.

" Did you make a search for it ? " asked Warwick.

" A did, sur ; a lukit iverywhaur, an' as suin as it wuz daylicht a walkit ower as far as Dillon's, thinkin' a micht hae drappit it on the road. But there wuz nae sign o' it."

" What's to be done ? " asked the colonel.

There was silence for a minute, and then Warwick spoke.

" Let us look at the matter in its worst possible light," he said. " I am the only one present who can be affected by the document, and then only in the event of my handwriting being recognised. Let us suppose the document to have fallen into the hands of Dillon, accidentally or otherwise. He is familiar with my handwriting. I am told he is my enemy. Why he should be so I cannot tell. He may be able to get a price from Government for that paper, and I may be arrested. That, however, would be all, I could not be punished for so trifling a matter,"

He spoke boldly, clearly, nay, even gaily, for he felt the trembling form of Mary by his side, and with a smile he whispered to her to fear nothing.

" Mr. Warwick," said Colonel Bryson, " my advice to you is to leave the country at once. You can easily make some pretext, and *when you are wanted we'll send for you.*"

As he spoke, hurried footsteps dashed up the close. A hand was laid upon the latch, the door was flung open, and a man entered, breathless and covered with perspiration from violent exercise. He made straight for the parlour, and, pointing to William Warwick, exclaimed—

" Rin an' hide yersel', sur, the sodgers ir lukin fur ye an' they'll be here in five minutes."

CHAPTER XIV.

THE YORK FENCIBLES.

" Stealthily they march along,
Under cover of the night,
Many hearts will troubled be
Ere they see to-morrow's light."—OLD BALLAD.

CONCEALED from observation by the darkness of the wintry evening, Dillon strode with rapid steps along the road leading to Newtownards. His hairy cap was drawn down over his ears ; the collar of his huge overcoat was turned up ; thus his features were completely hidden, and, as he pressed forward, cudgel in hand, he would have escaped recognition, even had the evening been a clearer one.

An English regiment—the York Fencibles—commanded by Colonel Stapleton, was stationed at Newtownards. The Colonel had his quarters in Conway Square and thither did Dillon turn his steps. He speedily gained admittance and learned that the Colonel was " at home."

" Give him that letter," said Dillon, " and say that the writer of it wishes to see him."

He had not long to wait. The colonel having glanced over the letter directed Dillon to be shown up, and the next moment they were face to face. The colonel eyed him keenly.

" Have you got this document with you ? " he asked.

" I have," said Dillon.

" Let me see it," said the colonel sharply, extending his hand.

Dillon hesitated.

" I want to see it," said Stapleton.

" But—the—reward— " stammered Dillon.

" Oh, never mind the reward ; that's a matter to be considered hereafter. Show me the paper."

Dillon drew the document from his pocket and handed it to the colonel, who sat down and perused it attentively.

Then he took up a pen and a sheet of paper.

" Your name ? " he asked, without looking at his visitor.

" James Dillon," replied that worthy.

" Your place of abode, and business ? "

Dillon replied to this and other questions.

The colonel wrote down his answers and pinned the sheet of paper containing them to the document stolen from Sam Donaldson. These he locked in a small writing case, and then rising to his feet said—

" You know, of course, where this fellow Warwick, lives ? "

" I do," replied Dillon.

" In half an hour a party of my men will start for his house. You must conduct them thither."

Dillon started. " Don't ask me to do that ! " he said.

"Why not ? " asked the colonel.

" My name must not appear in the matter, good or bad," said Dillon. " If it does I may leave the country at once."

" Humph ! " muttered the colonel, " you informers are all the same ; damned cowards, every one of you ! "

He stood for a minute or two biting his moustache and buried in thought. Then he asked—

" And how can my men find the place ? "

" I'll show it to them," said Dillon ; " I'll wait for them on the road and point it out."

" Very good ; be off with you ! "

But Dillon stood still. He did not quite like the colonel's manner, and fully expected to have his pockets filled with gold. The colonel divined his thoughts.

" You may go," he said ; when the case has been disposed of the Government will decide whether you are to be rewarded or not."

Dillon felt disappointed, but there was no help for it, so he turned and left, feeling anything but comfortable.

Twenty minutes later, half a dozen of the York Fencibles, wrapped in their great coats, and armed with muskets and bayonets, were tramping along the road leading to Drumawhey. The night was bitterly cold, and the sergeant in charge of the men growled fiercely against the ill-luck which had turned him out of his warm quarters.

Suddenly a man emerged from the hedge, and, facing the soldiers, held up his hand.

" Halt ! " cried the sergeant, " Who goes there ? "

" A friend," was the reply.

It was Dillon.

He whispered certain instructions to the sergeant, and then stole forward in advance of the party, creeping like a shadow along the hedgerow.

But another chapter is required to relate the doings of that night —a night ever to be remembered in Drumawhey.

CHAPTER XV.

ON THE TRACK.

" What strange foreboding fills the mother's breast ?
She sleeps, but, ah, how brief shall be her rest ! "

Widow Warwick sat in her old arm-chair by the turf fire, reading. The door was barred and the blinds down. A wiry-looking terrier was stretched at full length upon the hearth, enjoying to the full the grateful warmth of the blazing turf. The only sound within the cottage was the monotonous ticking of the old clock which hung upon the wall ; the only sound without was the moaning of the wintry wind.

Ever and anon did the widow's eyes turn towards the dial of that old clock, and then, with a sigh, she would resume her reading. But the book, whatever it was, failed to interest her ; by-and-by she closed it, and, leaning forward upon the little table placed near to her, she dropped asleep.

Her's was a rude awakening.

There was a quick, sharp snarl from the dog, as he sprang up and bounded towards the door ; a heavy tramp of feet without ; the crash of a musket butt upon the frail bar, and a shout of—

" Open, in the King's name ! "

Scarcely knowing what to think, with beating heart and shaking limbs, Mrs. Warwick staggered forward, withdrew the bar, raised the latch, and flung open the door.

The sergeant and his men stepped in, with quick military precision.

" Your name, my good woman ? " demanded the sergeant, as he faced the widow.

" Warwick, sir; Mrs. Warwick, sir," stammered the terrified woman.

" How many people are in this house ? " asked the soldier.

" I am alone, sir ; indeed, indeed I am," was the answer.

Where is your son ? "

" He left here this morning, and has not since returned."

" Do you expect him soon ? "

" I do not sir ; he said that he would be out late, and that I need not sit up for him."

The sergeant was not a bad fellow. Beneath a rugged exterior he had a kindly heart, and he was touched by the widow's pale face and appealing looks.

" What do you want my boy for ? " she sobbed.

" Treason, I dare say ; but my orders are to take him prisoner."

" Oh, soldier, dear ! " cried Mrs. Warwick, dropping before him upon her knees, " there must be some mistake ; my son guilty of treason. It cannot be ! "

" Here is my warrant, madam," said the sergeant, drawing a paper from his breast, " and the name is William Warwick—William Warwick of Drumawhey. Sorry to appear rude, but must obey orders."

Then turning to his men, he said—

" Let two remain outside ; the others search the house. Remember, no violence ! "

The sergeant had no heart for his work ; his men had. They demanded candles, and, having procured these, the search commenced.

Every apartment in the house, every bed, wardrobe, or other article of furniture likely to afford a hiding-place, was examined. Their man was not there.

Meantime Mrs. Warwick had somewhat recovered her composure. The thought had occurred to her of sending a messenger to Betsy Gray's house to warn William of his danger. But how could this be done ? She resolved to hazard the detention of the soldiers in order to gain time. She guessed they had some one as a spy who would guide them to where her son was.

" You see I told you the truth," she said to the sergeant in a reproachful tone, when the search was over.

" I did not doubt your word," he replied, " but a soldier must perform his duty, however unpleasant."

" And very unpleasant you must find such work to be," said the widow, " that is if you are a man of feeling. The night is cold, allow me to offer you and your men some refreshment."

" No, thanks," said the sergeant. But as he looked at his men he saw the disappointment caused by his answer. In his absence they would have helped themselves.

" Well," he said, " I see my men are cold ; a glass of punch will do them no harm."

" I cannot offer them whiskey," said Mrs. Warwick, " but if some hot milk with buttered oatcake and cheese would be acceptable—"

" The very thing ! " chorused the men, piling their arms in a corner and gathering round the fire.

Mrs. Warwick, with perfect self-possession, laid her table, which was soon surrounded by the men, who, judging by their appetites, must have been half-famished.

" My supply of milk has run short," apologised the hostess, " but I have a good neighbour who will lend me a couple of quarts till to-morrow."

" Your health, madam ! " cried the sergeant, cheerily, lifting his noggin of hot milk to his lips.

" Thank you," responded the widow, as she flung a shawl over her head and shoulders, and took up a milk pail from beneath the dresser.

The opportunity she sought had come ! The soldiers suspected nothing.

The distance to her nearest neighbour's was scarcely a hundred yards, but Mrs. Warwick thought it more than double that as she ran towards it at full speed. She lifted the latch and entered. There were but two inmates, John Simpson and his wife. Both started to their feet, alarmed by the woman's sudden entrance, and as the shawl fell from her white terror-striken face they exclaimed—

" What's wrang, Mrs. Warwick ? "

" Oh, dear," cried the widow, " the soldiers are looking for my son to arrest him. He is at Betsy Gray's party. John, run like lightning, take the short cut across the fields, and warn him to some hiding-place. For God's sake, hurry ! "

The man needed no urging. He seized his hat and stick and was off in a twinkling.

Then Mrs. Warwick, in quick, disjointed sentences, told her neighbour how matters stood, Mrs. Simpson supplied her pail, and the widow returned to her house to find her unwelcome guests enjoying themselves heartily.

Ten minutes later they had gone. She listened to the tramp of their feet till the sound died away in the distance. Then her fortitude deserted her. She burst into tears, and, falling upon her knees, pleaded in prayer for the life of her darling son.

* * * * * * * * * * *

The house of Dillon, the spy and informer, was not far from that of Mrs. Warwick.

He conducted the soldiers almost to the very door, and arranged with the sergeant that when he had made the arrest he should call with him (Dillon) and have a drink.

It was to Dillon's house, accordingly, that the soldiers went. They found the bar empty, as far as customers were concerned, a circumstance that was quite a relief to Dillon. That worthy showed the soldiers into the room reserved for visitors, and then he and the sergeant had a confidential chat. He told the sergeant what he had learned from his wife, namely, that William Warwick was spending the evening at Betsy Gray's, and he proposed that the sergeant, with his men, should proceed thither, where the arrest would be certain.

The sergeant demurred. The night was cold and the distance considerable.

" I prefer to wait here," he said, " for a few hours, until he returns home. Then we can capture our bird quietly."

This did not suit Dillon's views. He fancied he could see the little party broken up, and wished in his heart that he could be there as an onlooker.

" Look here, sergeant," he said, " this house of Gray's is a regular hot bed of treason and conspiracy. If you make a raid upon it you may catch more birds than one ; in fact, this night's work, if properly done, should secure your immediate promotion. Have a drink and think the matter over."

Whiskey, and plenty of it, was supplied to all hands. The men were nothing loth to drink it, and while they are so employed let us see how it fares with Warwick, who, as my readers have already learned, received timely warning from his neighbour, John Simpson. In those days the utmost terror prevailed. Outrages were hourly expected. Nearly every house had provided some sort of hiding place. There was a peculiar one at Betsy Gray's. A large turf stack was so constructed that, by withdrawing a few of the turf at a particular spot, entrance was gained to a hollow space capable of accommodating three or four persons. It was well lined with straw, and the ventilation was tolerably good. The place could not be regarded as very comfortable, but it was looked upon as safe.

" Come with me, Mr. Warwick," said George Gray, " and I'll see you to safe quarters."

With the utmost coolness George assisted Warwick to put on his top coat, then there was a hurried " good-night," and the two left the room.

Emerging from the kitchen by a back door, George led Warwick to the place of hiding, the nature of which had previously been known to him.

" We may be able to relieve you from your unpleasant quarters in the course of an hour." said George ; " meantime, fear nothing, you are absolutely safe."

" God bless you !" said Warwick, as he pressed his companion's hand.

In less time than is required to tell it, Warwick was coiled up in his strange retreat, and George had rejoined his friends in the parlour.

It was a considerable time before the soldiers arrived, and the period was one of trying anxiety to the little party, and to the women in particular. Mary Stewart was in a state bordering upon despair.

When the soldiers arrived, she fainted in Betsy's arms. Hans Gray held parley with the sergeant in the kitchen. The man was less civil now than before. He was maddened by Dillon's bad whiskey and indignant that he had arrived too late, after a cold and dirty march.

" Search the place ! " he said, as he turned to his men and struck the floor with the butt of his musket. " The damned rebel must be found ! "

The men went to work with a will. Tables were overturned ; beds and bed-clothes tossed upon the floors ; chests and presses burst open, amid a perfect babel of shouts and oaths.

The search was vain.

" Out with you !" shouted the leader; " search the outhouses, he may be in hiding there ! "

His order was obeyed instantly.

Seizing huge pieces of burning bogwood, which served as torches, the soldiers explored stable, barn, byre, and piggery. As they ran round the turf-stack, which stood at the rere of the house, and in which the man they sought was concealed, one of the soldiers was seized with a fiendish idea.

" I say, boys," he said, " what a jolly bonfire this turf-stack would make. I vote we burn it ! "

" Good, Ned," said another, " apply a light."

No sooner said than done.

Several of the flaming torches were at once applied.

The turf was dry, being well sheltered, and caught fire instantly.

A wild cheer burst from the soldiers at the prospect of a magnificent conflagration.

CHAPTER XVI.

OFF THE TRACK.

" Come weal, come woe, while this right hand
Can wield my broad sword, here I stand !" — LYTTLE.

THE shouts of the half-drunken soldiers brought their sergeant to the place where they were congregated. He was followed by the male inmates of the house, who feared that Warwick had been discovered. It is needless to say that the utmost alarm filled the hearts of Warwick's friends when they saw the position of affairs. The turf-stack had been lighted at the end farthest from the hiding place. This was in favour of the fugitive ; still, if the fire were allowed to proceed, his fate was certain. Either he would be roasted alive, or, rushing forth from his hiding place he would fall into the hands of his pursuers.

It was a critical moment.

With his usual impetuosity, George Gray rushed forward, while the others looked on horror-stricken.

Seizing the sergeant by the arm, he demanded —

" What means this outrage ? We have thrown no obstacle in the way of your search, and will you permit your men to burn our property ? "

" Certainly not ! " returned the sergeant, somewhat alarmed by the rashness of his men. " Who did this ? " he shouted.

No one replied.

" Out with the fire ! " cried the sergeant, and the men went to work kicking at the smouldering turf. Boal and his friends brought buckets of water, and in a few minutes the blaze was quenched. Then the sergeant re-formed his men and marched them off.

George Gray hastened to assure Warwick of his present safety, and cautioned him to lie perfectly still until he should return to him.

A consultation was then held by Warwick's friends, but they were divided in their opinions. Colonel Bryson suggested that he should sail from Donaghadee to Scotland, and remain there until sent for. George Gray was in favour of keeping him under cover in Granshaw, having trusty men to keep watch by day and night to give warning at the approach of danger.

" What do you say, Willie ? " asked Mr. Gray, turning to Boal, who had not yet spoken.

" Bring in Mr. Warwick and let him speak for himself," said Boal.

" Right ! " said George.

" But the soldiers may return," said Mary Stewart, who, pale and trembling, was listening to all that passed.

" Never fear ! " said George, " I'll see to that."

And so he did. A couple of trusty farm servants were so stationed that no one could approach the house unseen, and they perfectly understood their duty.

Warwick was then brought from his hiding-place to take part in the consultation. He listened attentively to all the suggestions his friends had to offer before he spoke a word touching himself.

" Well, Mr. Warwick, what is your own opinion ? " asked Bryson.

" I shall not leave the country," replied Warwick. " It would break my mother's heart to leave her. Besides, the offence which I have committed, if offence it is, is so very trifling that the punishment could not be great."

" I am not so sure of that," said Bryson. " A very slight offence just now is liable to be heavily punished, and I begin to think that none of us are safe. Would to God that the time for action had come, for then would there be an end of all this suspense, anxiety and uncertainty ! "

" The soldiers may return at any moment," whispered Mary Stewart.

"No, Mary," said Warwick, " there is no danger of that; after the thorough search which I am told they have made, they are not at all likely to return. And, indeed, I believe that, for a time, I would be perfectly safe either here or at my mother's house, provided I kept under cover."

" Then, what is your decision ? " asked George Gray.

" I remain here or go home," replied Warwick.

" Then here you shall remain," said George, " for you will be safer here than at home. It can easily be arranged to have timely notice given of the approach of strangers, and then we have your snug hiding place."

Warwick was correct in the opinion which he had formed. No further search was made for him, and the rumour was industriously circulated that be had left the country. His mother, the Grays, and a few trusty friends, alone knew of his whereabouts, and it is needless to say that they kept their secret well.

Several months elapsed without anything worthy of note having occurred to the personages who have, for so far, figured in this story. Secret meetings were held as usual, arms and ammunition were purchased and hidden away to be produced when wanted, and everything seemed to be in readiness for a general rising. In every district " warners " were appointed. It was the duty of these men to convey, from house to house the " call of arms " when the order to that effect should be issued. Many people left the country. Others who remained lived in terror of their lives. Rumours of the most awful natures were afloat. Not a few looked with disfavour upon the state of affairs, and had no desire to take up arms. It was openly stated that such persons would, when the rising took place, be regarded as enemies and treated as such.

Our Granshaw friends felt no fear. They never for a moment doubted that success would attend the United Irishmen, and they waited impatiently for the summons to the field.

The month of April had come, and Warwick was still in concealment. He had begun to regard himself as perfectly safe, and was tempted to lay aside his habits of caution. Under cover of night he frequently visited his mother.

On the occasion of one of these visits, while in his mother's house, there came on a violent storm of wind and rain. Mrs. Warwick begged of her son not to expose himself to the fury of the elements, and so the two sat hour after hour talking of their plans and prospects. At length it was decided that he should remain all night and next day, returning to Granshaw on the following night.

Warwick went to his little bedroom and slept soundly. His mother had led him to believe that she also would retire to bed. She did not do so. Like the devoted mother that she was she sat up all through the long night, keeping watch over her only son.

The visit proved to be an unfortunate one !

CHAPTER XVII.

THE WIDOW'S CURSE.

" A wicked deed, in truth, a wicked deed,
For this my country's heart shall one day bleed !"—LYTTLE.

DILLON'S connection with the pursuit of Warwick was known only to himself, his wife, and the military authorities. There were many persons who did not hesitate to hint at the suspicions which were entertained, but nothing had as yet transpired to confirm those suspicions.

Mrs. Warwick supplied several of her neighbours with milk and butter. Dillon's wife was one of her customers, and on the morning which succeeded the night dealt with in the preceding chapter, Mrs. Dillon, who was a coarse-minded, uneducated woman, went to Mrs. Warwick's house for some buttermilk. Her visit was a fatal one to Warwick. He was up, had breakfasted, and had written a note which he meant to send over to Betsy Gray.

A door opened from Mrs. Warwick's kitchen into a hall, or passage, which led to the other apartments. The upper portion of the door was glass. Warwick had just reached this door with the object of speaking to his mother in the kitchen at the very moment of Mrs. Dillon's entrance. He retreated instantly, but the quick eye of Dillon's wife caught a glimpse of the retreating figure. She noted too, the nervousness displayed by Mrs. Warwick, who, poor soul, could scarcely measure out the milk.

Mrs. Dillon returned home in great glee.

" A hae news fur ye this mornin', Jamey ! " she exclaimed, as she entered the house and put down her can of milk.

" What is it ? " queried Dillon.

" *A think there's a rat in the trap !* " said the woman, speaking slowly and significantly.

" A what ? " cried Dillon, now thoroughly aroused.

His wife related what had transpired, and concluded her story by repeating the words — " *A think there's a rat in the trap !* "

" There must be no *thinking* about it," said Dillon ; " you must make sure of it. Go back and discover what you can."

" What excuse can a mak' ? " asked the woman.

" Any excuse you like," said Dillon, becoming quite excited " here, empty your can and go back for more milk."

As he spoke he lifted the can, emptied the contents into a crock, handed her the empty vessel, and in his eagerness pushed her out by the shoulders.

Mrs. Warwick seemed slightly surprised at the sudden return of her customer, but she had no suspicion of the nature of her errand.

" Can ye spare me twa quarts mair buttermilk ? " asked Mrs. Dillon.

" Certainly," replied Mrs. Warwick, stepping towards the churn.

But her customer's next remark rooted her to the floor —

" Whun did Mester William cum hame ? "

The widow was speechless for several moments, then she faltered —

" Do you mean my son ? "

" Ay," said Mrs. Dillon ; " didn't a see him through the gless daur the last time a cummed in ? "

The widow made no reply. Lifting a piece of butter weighing several pounds, she placed it in the bottom of the can, poured the buttermilk over it, and handing the vessel with its contents to Mrs. Dillon, said significantly —

" *There's a small present for you.*"

Poor Mrs. Warwick ! She thought her simple bribe would secure the silence of her customer.

Mrs. Dillon, with a dry " Thank ye," took her butter and milk and departed. Then the widow slipped the bar in the door, and rushing down to her son's bedroom, exclaimed —

" William, dear, you have been seen ! "

" By whom ? " he asked, starting.

" Dillon's wife."

" The worst may be expected then," said Warwick. " Mother, dear " he continued, rising and taking his mother's hands, " I believe Dillon to be a spy and an informer. We must get some place of hiding in readiness."

The mother's grief was pitiable to behold. Her son comforted her as best he could, and, to please him, she affected a composure she was far from feeling.

Meantime, Dillon had learned from his wife all that had passed between her and Mrs. Warwick. He gave instructions to have the house watched, and instantly started off for Newtownards, where he acquainted the military authorities of Warwick's whereabouts, and, returning home, awaited the result.

It so happened that the same sergeant who had been sent to arrest Warwick on a previous occasion was again entrusted with the commission. He took with him a number of men, and, in the course of an hour from the time of receiving orders, was at the house.

The search was rapid, but thorough, and was carried out without any unnecessary violence.

Warwick was not discovered.

The sergeant marched his men straight to Dillon's public house, where they filed in.

" Have you been there ? " asked Dillon.

" Yes, I have," replied the sergeant, " and another wild goose chase it's been."

" I'll swear he's there ! " shouted Dillon, bringing down his fist with a heavy thud upon the counter.

" Then you'll find him for us ! " said the sergeant.

" What do you mean ? " asked Dillon.

" Just this," said the sergeant, " You say the man's there. I say we searched for and failed to find him ; now, you come along with us and pick him up."

Dillon turned pale.

" Indeed I won't !" he said.

" By G—d you shall ! " exclaimed the sergeant. " Do you think I have got to run over this damned place to amuse you ? Turn out now, or I'll blow your cowardly brains out ! "

As he spoke he drew a pistol and placed the muzzle against the informer's head. Dillon looked straight into the sergeant's eyes. There was no doubt that the man was in earnest.

" Put down your weapon ; I'll go," said Dillon.

" I should think you will ! " said the sergeant, as he replaced his pistol. " Come along instantly."

There was no help for it, and the next minute the soldiers, accompanied by Dillon, were retracing their steps towards Warwick's house.

The news had gone abroad and a small crowd had collected. When the people saw Dillon in company with the military they at first supposed he had been placed under arrest, and they expressed considerable surprise. Following at a respectable distance, they learned the true state of affairs.

The house was soon reached, and Dillon, seeing that there was no help for it, took the lead. He led the soldiers straight to Warwick's bedroom. As he entered he noticed, or fancied that he noticed, a slight flutter of the curtain which hung between the bed and the wall.

It was not a fancy !

" Did you look here ? " asked Dillon, stepping forward and drawing aside the curtain.

Warwick stood revealed !

A hideous grin overspread the face of the informer as he turned to the sergeant and said—

" *I have found the blackbird !*"

Warwick stepped from his hiding place, pale but undaunted.

" Are you William Warwick ? " asked the sergeant.

" I am ! " he replied,

" Then I arrest you in the King's name ! "

At this moment Warwick's mother flung herself into her son's arms and burst into a fit of weeping.

Warwick's lips quivered.

" Don't cry, mother," he said, as he gently stroked her grey hair. " Bear up, good mother, there shall no harm befall me."

Then his eye fell upon Dillon, and drawing himself up to his full height, he said—

" And this is *your* work, Dillon ! "

The fellow made no answer, but slunk back, as though ashamed of the position he occupied.

Warwick looked at him steadily for a moment ; then, pointing his finger upward, said solemnly—

" There will be a day of reckoning, Dillon ; when that day comes may God forgive you as I do ! "

The words aroused his mother. Unwinding her arms from her son's neck, she turned upon Dillon with fierce glaring eyes.

" Forgive him ! " she cried. " Never ! God will never forgive such a wretch ! May you never know peace ! May the hand of an avenging God fall upon you ! May the curse of a widowed mother follow you to your dying day ! "

Her outstretched arms fell by her side ; a shiver passed through her frame, and she sank back fainting in the arms of her son.

CHAPTER XVIII.

SENTENCE OF DEATH.

" The dreadful fierceness of thy wrath
quite over me doth go ;
Thy terrors great have cut me off,
they did pursue me so." —PSALM.

WARWICK was dragged away from his unconscious mother and conducted, a prisoner, to Newtownards. A Court-martial was held in the markethouse there, with Lord Londonderry as President, and before this court the unhappy Warwick was brought.

He was formally charged with having issued a treasonable document. Witnesses there were none. Dillon could not be induced either by threats or promises, to appear, and he alone was responsible for the arrest.

The deliberation was brief. In reply to the President, Warwick acknowledged that the paper was in his handwriting.

The verdict was speedily found.

It was a verdict of GUILTY.

Lord Castlereagh asked the prisoner if he had anything to say in his defence.

" Yes, my lord, and gentlemen, I have," said Warwick, drawing up his fine figure to its full height. " I have to ask, nay, to demand, that my accusers all be brought before me. Is this the boasted justice of our country ? Are we to be at the mercy of any unprincipled and mercenary scoundrel who chooses to traffic in human blood ? Where is Dillon ? Produce him ! Let *him* say what evidence is against me. I have admitted that that document is in my handwriting, but I am not responsible for the framing of it. I did not dream that in making a copy from the original I was placing my life in peril, or erring in my loyalty to the King. I have no more to say ! "

" Who asked you to make a copy of the document ? " asked Castlereagh.

The prisoner did not reply.

" If you make a full disclosure of all the circumstances," continued Castlereagh, " giving us the names and addresses of all parties implicated in this matter, I shall see that a favourable representation of your case is made to his Excellency the Lord Lieutenant, and your life may probably be spared."

" Is it, then, a matter of life or death ? Be it so, my lord ; I am prepared to die, young as I am and with all the world before me, but I am NOT prepared to imperil the life or liberty of any other human being ! "

Sentence of death was immediately passed, and Warwick was led away by the military to a place of confinement. There he was left alone.

What tongue could tell the agony endured by the unfortunate prisoner during the weary hours of that day ? Every footstep that sounded upon his ear he fancied might be the summons to the gallows, for in those days execution followed swiftly upon the sentence. His mother ? What of her ? His betrothed—his darling Mary—what of her ? He thought not of himself ; of the shameful death he was to die—every thought was of his mother, his sweetheart, and his friends.

" Oh, God ! " he exclaimed, dropping upon his knees, and wringing his hands in agony, " if it be Thy will, let my life be spared, if only for a little. Let not mine enemies cut me off thus suddenly. Pity the widow, and spare her only son ! "

Then he sat down on the comfortless bed which his cell contained, and drawing from his pocket a Bible, he opened it, as though to seek comfort from its pages. His eye fell upon the 88th Psalm, and as he read it, every line seemed to have been penned for his especial case.

Food and water were brought to him, but he could not partake of them. Night came, but he could not sleep, and the dawn found him tossing upon his sleepless pillow.

A key turned in the lock ; there was a sound of footsteps, and the sergeant who had arrested him stood by his side.

Warwick started up.

" Is it time ? " he exclaimed.

" For what ? " asked the sergeant.

" For my execution ! " said Warwick.

" No, Mr. Warwick," said the sergeant, in a kindly voice, " I have come to tell you that your life may be spared."

The prisoner sprang to his feet and caught the sergeant's hands in his own.

" Let me not raise false hopes," the sergeant continued, " but I must tell you what I know. Mr. Warwick, I pity your mother, and I cannot help feeling admiration for yourself. Several members of the court-martial were in favour of an acquittal, and a statement of your case has been forwarded to the Lord Lieutenant, who may consider it with favour. Now, bear up ; take your breakfast when it is brought, and after that, if I can have any message conveyed to your friends I shall do so."

" May heaven bless you ! " said Warwick, fervently.

" I must go," said the sergeant, as he turned abruptly and left.

He was not a bad fellow. His eye was moist as he traversed the passage leading from the prisoner's cell.

It was at this moment that the thirteenth verse of the 88th Psalm rose before Warwick's mental vision—

" But unto Thee have I cried, O Lord ; and in the morning shall my prayer prevent Thee."

A sudden calm pervaded his bosom ; he stretched himself upon his prison bed, and in a few minutes was fast asleep.

CHAPTER XIX.

THE SAINTFIELD INFORMER.

" And the Rev. Cleland did think it no sin
To plot with that sneaking informer, Maginn." —OLD BALLAD.

IN a wretched dwelling, in a lonely locality, not far from Saintfield, dwelt Nick Maginn. He was miserably poor, and of miserly habits. Partly from curiosity, partly from fear, and partly from hope of gain, he had joined the United Irishmen. He possessed a remarkable memory in certain respects. Words and figures repeated to him he could remember with singular accuracy. His talent in this respect he turned to advantage.

Maginn soon made the discovery that the informers would be the best paid people amongst the rebels, and no sooner had he made that discovery than he decided upon being an informer. Chance threw him in the way of a reverend person named James Cleland,

and the two were well met. If history speaks truly, Cleland was as little caring for the means he used to obtain information as Maginn was.

At this period the popularity of the Rev. William Steele Dickson was unbounded. His fiery eloquence, his manly bearing, his fearless nature, and the power which he wielded, unconsciously, over the people, pointed him out as one suitable to lead them in the coming struggle.

One night, just about the time of Warwick's arrest, Maginn was sitting by his miserable hearth, cowering over the faint heat emitted by a few dried twigs gathered from the neighbouring hedges. His skinny hands were extended over the smouldering fire, and as he now and then rubbed them slowly together, he chuckled inwardly, as though brooding over some subject which afforded him gratification.

Frequently, very frequently, his eye turned to the aged and dirt-begrimed clock that hung upon the wall, as though he waited for the hands to indicate a certain hour.

And so he did.

The hour at length arrived, and Maginn rose from the fire, buttoned his threadbare coat, took up a stout blackthorn cudgel, and left the house, fastening the door behind him.

On this particular occasion Nick had an appointment with the Rev. James Cleland and that worthy now sat at the house of a friend, less than a mile distant, awaiting Maginn's arrival.

Cleland was the established clergyman in Newtownards and a magistrate, as well as being an agent of Lord Londonderry.

Our Saintfield hero was true to his appointment, and was announced at the very minute that Cleland had remarked to his friend — " He should be here now."

Maginn was shown into an apartment, where he was speedily joined by his clerical acquaintance. He pulled his forelock as the clergyman entered.

" Well, Maginn," said his reverence, " any news to-night? "

" Oh, ay ; there's a bit sough gaun here as usual."

" But anything definite ? "

" Anythin' what ? " asked Maginn, stupidly. The word " definite " was beyond his comprehension.

" Have you heard any date named for a rising ? " asked Cleland.

" Na, a hae not; but it micht be ony minit."

" Is that all you can tell me ? " queried Cleland with a look of disappointment.

Maginn looked around cautiously, and then asked—

" Can onybuddy hear us ? "

" No," replied Cleland, opening the door, and again closing it ; " we are entirely alone and safe from interruption."

Still Maginn hesitated.

" Have you anything to tell me ? " asked Cleland.

" A hae," said Maginn. " but luk here, yer reverince, if it wuz kent that a wuz carryin' news tae you a wud be blawn tae smithereens. A wud niver gang hame this nicht alive."

" Never fear, my man," replied Cleland, assuringly ; " you are perfectly safe in communicating everything that you know to me, and your reward is certain."

Maginn chuckled.

" Hoo muckle wull a get ? " he asked.

" That depends upon the nature of the information you give, " said his reverence.

" Weel, then, a shud get a guid dale," replied Maginn, " fur a think a can pit ye on the track o' wha's to be General in command ! "

" Ha ! " cried Cleland, " Who is he ? "

Again Maginn's caution returned, and he looked around suspiciously. Then crossing the room to where Cleland stood, he whispered in his ear—

" Mister Steele Dickson ! "

The announcement appeared to take Cleland completely by surprise. He stood for several minutes absolutely speechless, then a smile of satisfaction lit up his face.

" You are sure of this, Maginn ? " he asked, eagerly.

" As shair as a'm a leevin' man."

" Good ! " exclaimed Cleland.

He paced the room for a minute, buried in thought, then turning to his companion, he said—

" Maginn, if your information proves to be correct, you shall indeed merit a large reward, and you may rely upon my word that you will receive it. Tell me, now, how came you to obtain this information, for we must act with caution, and be sure of the nature of the ground upon which we tread. Will you have a glass of whiskey ? "

Maginn drew the back of his hand across his mouth and nodded assent. His reverence produced a decanter and tumbler, and having helped his guest freely, sat down.

Maginn refreshed the inner man and then proceeded to unbosom himself, while his reverend companion listened eagerly, now and then taking notes in his pocket book.

Let us leave the worthy pair so occupied, and turn to other personages more deserving of attention.

CHAPTER XX.

REV. WILLIAM STEELE DICKSON.

" A man of generous heart and noble mind !
A man whose like we ne'er again may find." — LYTTLE.

NUMEROUS clergymen in the County of Down took an active part in the movement of 1798 — and suffered for it. Prominent amongst these was the Rev. William Steele Dickson, at that period a minister of the Presbyterian Church in Portaferry. Mr. Dickson was born on Christmas Day, 1744, at Ballycraigy, in the parish of Carnmoney. His father John Dickson, was a farmer. His mother's name was Jane Steele. William, in his early boyhood, gave evidence of talent, and attracted the notice of the Rev. Robert White, minister of Templepatrick (a parish adjoining Carnmoney), who, taking a fancy to the lad, imparted to him a considerable part of his early education.

At the age of seventeen William Steele Dickson entered Glasgow College, without having any definite views as to what his future course of life should be. Under the training of two of the college professors, the celebrated Adam Smith and John Millar, he devoted his attention chiefly to law and politics. It was from Millar that he derived the germ of his political creed. Having finished his undergraduate course, young Dickson was influenced by his early instructor and pastor, Mr. White, to become a Presbyterian Minister, and, having gone through the prescribed course, he was licensed to preach in the month of March, 1767. It was four years before he received a " call," and during this period he preached as a probationer, being frequently sent as an occasional supply to various congregations, and thus becoming acquainted with many prominent families in the counties of Antrim and Down. Amongst these was the family of Alexander Stewart, of Londonderry, and grandfather of the notorious Lord Castlereagh.

The year 1771 was an important one in Dickson's life. In that year (on 6th March) he was ordained to the charge of the congregation of Ballyhalbert, County Down, and he also became a husband and a father. In Ballyhalbert he quickly acquired popularity. One of his earliest sermons preached there was against cock-fighting, and the practice was at once stopped.

On the 14th November, 1779, Mr. Dickson, by request, preached a funeral sermon at Portaferry, on the occasion of the death of the Rev. James Armstrong, the late minister of the Presbyterian congregation in that town. Such was the impression created by Mr. Dickson upon the members of the Portaferry congregation that they shortly after invited him to accept their vacant pulpit. He accepted that invitation, and was duly installed to the charge in March, 1780. About this time he began to take a warm interest in political affairs. In 1783, when Robert Stewart (afterwards the first Lord Londonderry) stood for the parliamentary representation of County Down, Dickson laboured most energetically on his behalf. He rode into Downpatrick at the head of about forty freeholders and well-to-do farmers. They were on horseback, and paraded the town in Indian file, after which Dickson formed them two deep and drew them up in front of Stewart's lodgings. All voted for Stewart. Later on, in 1789, there was another election held for County Down, and on this occasion the younger Stewart (afterwards Lord Castlereagh) was a candidate. Again did Dickson exert himself, this time with success, and such was his influence and popularity that in the year 1798 this very Castlereagh urged the arrest of Dickson, alleging that it would be dangerous to leave at liberty a man who was so popular amongst the people. But I am anticipating.

It was in the year 1791 that Dickson took the first step upon what turned out for him to be a dangerous road. In the December of that year he was sworn in as a United Irishman at Belfast, by the first society there formed. From the period of his initiation he became an active member, and was a leading speaker at numerous public meetings of the organisation.

In 1796, such was the estimation in which Dickson was held by the United Irishmen generally, that he was appointed Adjutant-General of the United Irish Forces for County Down. He was a courted and honoured guest in the houses of the wealthy merchants of Belfast, where his sparkling wit kept the table in a roar. His presence as a preacher was ever welcome, crowded audiences listening with delight to his burning eloquence. But with all this, he was not unmindful of his congregation in Portaferry, and he often declared that his happiest hours were spent by the firesides of the farmers in various portions of the Ards.

As might be expected, Dickson had his enemies, and many efforts were made to destroy his popularity. In October, 1796, a most determined attack was made upon his congregation. A poor man named Carr, in hope of reward, conveyed certain information to Colonel Savage, of Portaferry. This was quickly carried to Lord Castlereagh, who at once ordered the arrest of several of Dickson's most respected hearers. They were confined for a night in Portaferry and removed next day to Dublin, and Carr for safety lodged in Kilmainham, he, with his wife and family, being comfortably supported. It was hoped that Carr's evidence would lead to the arrest of Dickson also, and that gentleman was urged to seek refuge in flight. This he refused to do, and every week until the end of December he visited his imprisoned hearers—a circumstance which increased the hostility of his foes against him.

And here an incident may be related as illustrative of the measures taken by the minions of the Government to secure the conviction of certain suspects. Dickson, having occasion to go to Dublin, visited a number of gentlemen from Belfast who were then prisoners in Kilmainham. Here he learned that Carr, the informer, was in solitary confinement ; that he was frequently visited by people from Dublin Castle, and treated with great severity, *because his information fell short of his promise !* The unfortunate creature was, at times, nearly distracted from a sense of his guilt, and the condition of his wife and children, whom his tempters had then abandoned, and he felt that he would not prosecute, *to conviction*, a single individual against whom he had sworn.

Dickson enquired how this could be ascertained, and was informed that, if he chose, be could hear it from Carr's own lips.

" By all means let me hear it ! " said Dickson.

One of the prisoners (Smith) immediately left the place in which the interview was being held, and, returning in a few minutes, said—

" Come with me, Dickson ; the yard is clear."

Smith, Dickson, and another prisoner adjourned to the jail yard.

" Keep close to the wall here, " said Smith to Dickson, who did as directed.

Then Smith took a ball from his pocket, and, after various trials, succeeded in throwing it through a window over the spot where Dickson stood.

It was Carr's cell, and the man, who understood the signal, threw back the ball, and speaking from the window, asked what was wanted.

" Any news ? " enquired Smith.

" Na, no a word," answered Carr.

" No hope of your release ? "

" No a bit. It wuz the black day fur me that a said a cud gie my infumashin aboot dacent men. Oh, dear ! Oh, dear ! What am a tae dae, an' my wife an' weans stervin' ? "

For a length of time Carr went on lamenting his condition ; telling what he had done, and what he had suffered. The tale was an infamous one !

" Tell me, do you know the Rev. Mr. Steele Dickson ? " asked Smith.

" A dae," said Carr, " an' he's as dacent a gentleman as iver brauk breid."

" Isn't he a United Irishman ? "

" A'm tell't he is."

" Don't you know him to be one ? Have you ever met him at any of their meetings ? "

" Niver in my life," said Carr. " Nor a niver heerd o' him bein' seen at any."

" Haven't you been promised money if you would give information that would lead to his conviction ? "

Carr did not reply.

" Don't be afraid," said Smith, " we are prisoners like yourself, and you know I have promised to help you, if it be in my power to do so."

After another pause Carr said—

" *A wus promised a thoosan' pun' if a wud sweer against Mr. Dickson tae convict him !* "

* * * * * * * * * * *

Dickson bore cheering news from Kilmainham to his friends in Downpatrick Jail. They were tried at the following assizes and released.

The Rev. James Cleland was one of Dickson's bitterest enemies. That clerical celebrity had been tutor to Lord Castlereagh. It would, perhaps, be more accurate to say that he was Castlereagh's *footman*. Many people in those days spoke of him as " master of the croppy-hounds, pointers and terriers." He was subsequently vicar of Newtownards. Cleland exhibited remarkable zeal in the prosecution of Dickson's friends, and was not a little chagrined at their release.

"He planted the right . . . under Dillon's left jaw"
See Page 79.

He had hoped for great things from Carr, but was bitterly disappointed. As will be seen by the previous chapter, Cleland had found another tool in the person of Nick Maginn, of Saintfield.

The Clelands built Stormount Castle out of their gains, and are buried under an imposing monument at Dundonald. They had much trouble and sorrow laid on them.

At the time of the interview, already related, between Cleland and Maginn, Dickson was in Scotland, where he had been on a visit to his wife's uncle, from early in the previous March. He left Scotland in April and landed in Donaghadee. Having sent his servant on to Portaferry with his luggage, Dickson turned his steps towards Granshaw, with a view to visit the Grays and other friends in that neighbourhood.

CHAPTER XXI.

A MARE'S NEST.

" Conscience makes cowards of us all !"

JOHN DAVIS, Dickson's servant, pushed on from Donaghadee towards Portaferry, glad at his master's return and dreaming of no harm. A surprise was in store for him.

John reached the ancient little town in safety and had come near to the Market-house where he was surrounded by a number of soldiers, who made him a prisoner and carried him and his master's luggage to the guard-house. The scrutiny of the baggage which then took place was so minute as to excite the ridicule of the officers who stood by looking on. Everything in which aught of a dangerous character was likely to be concealed was tossed, shaken and turned outside in.

Suddenly something which emitted a sharp metallic sound fell upon the pavement,

" Ha !" exclaimed a soldier " what is that ? "

The others started back.

It was small box manufactured of steel and almost completely covered with rust.

Very suspicious, indeed, it looked !

What could it be ?

That it was an instrument of destruction all were agreed.

After the lapse of some time one of the soldiers more courageous than the rest, picked it up. His courage was applauded by the others who, somewhat ashamed of their conduct, now gathered round him.

The man strove to open it, but in vain. One after another tried, with a like result.

" Fetch a hammer ! " cried he who first seized the box. " I'll smash the damned thing ! It must contain a hidden spring ! "

While some one went in search of a hammer, Captain Marshall, who had been an amused spectator of the scene, stepped forward and lifted the box.

" Look here," he said, " it is the rust that prevents you from opening it. Hand me a knife."

Half a dozen pocket knives were quickly tendered. Taking one of these, the captain scraped off a quantity of rust, inserted the edge of the knife at the proper place, and the infernal machine flew open.

It was a tobacco box !

There was a hearty laugh, in which the discomfited soldiers joined and honest John was permitted to depart in peace.

The seizure of Dickson's luggage is easily accounted for. Maginn, the informer, had volunteered to Cleland the information that Dickson had gone to Scotland to form and promote there Societies of United Irishmen.

The story was a pure invention.

As for the infernal machine, Dickson tells the particulars connected with it in a book which he afterwards wrote and published. The tobacco box was a very large one. It had formerly belonged to a sea captain. On its being shown to Dickson, he admired it as a curiosity, became the possessor of it, and brought it with him to Ireland.

Cleland and Maginn were deeply disappointed by the result of the raid made upon Dickson's effects. They applied themselves with renewed energy to the object which they had in view, and the reverend gentleman was placed under close watch. His every step was dogged. What success attended the efforts of these base and treacherous creatures—these human blood-hounds—will but too soon be made apparent.

CHAPTER XXII.

A PUGILISTIC ENCOUNTER.

" A joke's a joke, but there's nae joke in that !
As Jamey Dillon said tae sturdy Mat."—OLD BALLAD.

FROM the day of Warwick's arrest Drumawhey became uncomfortable quarters for the informer Dillon.

His business dwindled away ; the few customers who called and drank his vile whiskey did so from curiosity to see the man chiefly. As for his school, it was completely broken up.

Dillon thought that in a short time the affair would blow over ; he would be comforted by a handsome Government reward, and his neighbours' tongues would be silenced, while his improved financial circumstances would obtain for him at all events a show of friendly feeling in the district.

Not many days passed ere he had an instance of the depth of the indignation which he had stirred amongst the people.

He wanted some trifling bit of smith-work done, and, throwing on his coat, he stepped across to his old acquaintance, Mat M'Clenaghan.

He found several men in the smiddy and around the door, engaged in conversation. Not one of these men so much as nodded to Dillon, or responded in any way to his salutation, given in a tone of forced cheerfulness.

" Well, Mat," he said, stepping inside, " that's a fine bracing day."

" Weel, ye hae yer share o' it," was the dry response.

Dillon did not appear to notice the reply or its tone, but, drawing from his pocket a piece of iron chain explained to Mat what he wanted done.

Mat looked at him sullenly, and went on with his work.

" I can wait till you have finished what you are at," said Dillon.

Mat laid down his hammer, and, looking Dillon straight in the face, said—

" If ye wait till a lift a hemmer fur you ye'll stan' there till doomsday."

" Nonsense ! " said Dillon, forcing a laugh ; my money's as good as other people's."

" It's naethin' o' the sort ! " said Mat, whose temper was rapidly rising.

" How is that ? " asked Dillon.

" Ye ken very weel athoot me tellin' ye," said Mat. " If ye want a chain tae tie *yersel'* tae a stake, a'll fix it fur ye, but yer dirty money wull niver gang in my pokit."

" Why do you speak to me in that way ? " said Dillon, in turn growing angry.

Mat threw down his hammer, and, stepping up to Dillon, said—

" Bekase ye hae nae biziness here."

" Mebbe he's lukin' fur pikes," said one of the bystanders.

This was a home-thrust, and Dillon, naturally a passionate man, became angry.

Turning round to the person who had made the remark, he said—

" And if I wanted pikes, my man, I think I wouldn't have far to look for them."

" An' if ye wud find ony here, " said Mat, " ye wud hae anither errand tae Newton fur the sodgers."

" What do ye mean ? " said Dillon.

"A mean this," said Mat; " the sodgers wuz here yince lukin' fur pikes, an' a hae a strong notion that you sent them. At ony rate ye tuk them tae his honour, Mr. Warwick."

" I merely did my duty," said Dillon, sullenly.

" Very likely," said Mat, drily. " There's fowk fur a' sorts o' bizziness, an' a suppoas the informin' bizziness pays best an' suits you. A hope a'll leeve tae see yer ugly neck streetched, ye ill-begotten, ugly lukin' bluid sucker ye !"

This was more than Dillon could stand. He lost his temper instantly, and, clenching his fist, he deliberately struck Mat in the face.

Several of the bystanders rushed forward to interfere, but the blacksmith, by a motion of his hand, restrained them.

Then he coolly took off his apron and threw it upon the anvil.

" Noo, Dillon," he said, " a didnae mean tae dirty my han's on ye, but as ye struck the first blow, a'll hae a slap back at ye. Cum ootside here, an' these dacent men wull see that ye'll get fair play."

Dillon saw his error, but it was too late to retreat. He felt confident he could easily defeat M'Clenaghan, so he stepped outside and stripped off his coat and waistcoat.

At the first glance Dillon seemed more than a match for Mat. He was a big-boned, muscular man. Mat was short in stature, but his daily work had developed the muscles of his arms to perfection, and his hands were hard as iron. Neither of the men knew aught of scientific pugilism, of the so-called noble art of self-defence. It was to be a question of punishment and their looks plainly denoted that the fight would be one to the finish.

The neighbours gathered round the contestants, but not a word was spoken.

" Noo, Dillon," cried Mat.

As he spoke, the two men met with a rush. Mat delivered the first blow, with fearful force, right upon Dillon's mouth, receiving in return one upon his chest.

The blood spurted from Dillon. He drew back, paused for a moment to wipe it with his shirt sleeve, and then made a second dash at his opponent.

Mat was not taken unawares, but from this until the finish the fighting was fast and furious. Dillon had a fancy for mad rushes, and he struck out wildly. Mat stood quietly on the defensive ; received the rushes from his opponent steadily, and delivered his blows with the force of a sledge hammer.

It was evident that the fight would be a short one. Dillon had measured the sod three times, and as yet Mat had not been knocked off his pins.

As the pair faced each other for the fourth time, Dillon chose to indulge in a bit of cautious sparring, evidently in the hope of landing a blow with effect. Mat determined to finish the business at once. Making a feint with his left, which somewhat threw his opponent off his guard, he planted the right with terrific force under Dillon's left jaw. The sound of the blow might have been heard at a considerable distance. Dillon went down like a felled ox, and lay motionless.

" Ye hae killed him, Mat," was the cry, as the spectators crowded around.

" Nae fear o' that! " laughed Mat, " The fellow's born tae be hung."

Dillon was not killed. A dash of cold water in his face brought him round ; he rose to his feet slowly and with a dazed look.

" Hae ye got eneuch ? " asked Mat.

Dillon made no answer, but proceeded to put on his hat, coat and vest. The next moment he slunk off, followed by the jeers and groans of the half-dozen men who had witnessed the fight.

Mat was never again troubled by a visit from the Drumawhey informer.

CHAPTER XXIII.

A SURPRISE.

" The dead alive again ! Can this be so ?
The future's hid from man, and well 'tis so."—ANON.

THE tidings communicated to the Rev. William Steele Dickson, when he arrived at Betsy Gray's house, filled him with sorrow and alarm. The poor girl was distracted with grief, and the clergyman's efforts to comfort her were vain.

" Do not weep, my good girl," said Dickson, laying his hand gently upon Betsy's head. " I feel sure that our friend Mr. Warwick will be set at liberty. He has committed no crime ; there is no evidence against him."

" What do you now think of James Dillon ? " asked Betsy.

" Indeed, Betsy, I am not by any means astonished," replied Dickson. " I never had a high opinion of him. Dear me ! How many people, after all, are not to be trusted in this world."

" He will surely come to a bad end," said Betsy, bitterly.

" We must not judge others, dear," said the minister, in a tone of gentle reproach. " There will, however, be a reward for all of us hereafter, according to the manner in which we have lived."

" Yes, Mr. Dickson, I know that," said Betsy. " But have you not seen these rewards coming to some people during their lives ? "

" Yes, Betsy, I have. We read, too, of many who have, apparently, drawn down upon themselves the avenging hand of God."

" Then Dillon shall be one of those ! " said Betsy, fiercely.

" Hush, my girl," whispered the minister ; " let us hope for his repentance."

" Ah, Mr. Dickson, if you saw poor Mrs. Warwick," said Betsy, the tears starting to her eyes. " She weeps and laments all day and night. No one can comfort her."

" I am truly sorry for her," said Dickson. " I shall go to her at once. After that I shall proceed to Newtownards and learn how fares our friend William."

" You will send us speedy news, won't you ? " said Mary Stewart, pleadingly.

" I shall indeed," he said. " Perhaps I shall bring you news personally."

Dickson partook of some refreshment and rose to leave. He had shaken hands with Betsy and advanced to where Mary Stewart was sitting.

" Be comforted ! " he said. " This is your first trial, and it is a very severe one. Remember the old saying that the darkest hour is before dawn. Rest assured, also, that no effort shall be spared to secure Mr. Warwick's immediate release."

Just at that instant Mary started to her feet and exclaimed excitedly—

" Betsy ! whose voice is that ? Run to the Kitchen. Quick ! " Betsy darted forward and opened the room door. As she did so, the tall, fine figure of a man pressed past her, and the next instant Mary Stewart was locked in William Warwick's arms.

" My darling ! " he murmured, " I am with you again."

Hurried explanations followed. Warwick had been reprieved. He did not tell them all, but he spoke cheerfully, and expressed the firm belief that he would shortly be entirely free.

Betsy went to the kitchen to have her father and brother sent for. She was horrified to find two soldiers sitting at the fire.

With pale face and frightened aspect the girl darted back to the parlour.

" Mr. Warwick ! " she exclaimed, " there are two —— men (she feared to say soldiers in Mary's hearing) in the kitchen."

" Don't be alarmed," said Warwick, laughing, " I should have explained that, but in the excitement of meeting you all I forgot. Those soldiers in the kitchen —— "

" Soldiers !" gasped Mary.

" Yes," said Warwick, " they are my guard of honour. At all events they are to accompany me wherever I go, day and night."

" What is that for ? " asked Mr. Dickson.

" To see that I do not escape," answered Warwick. " They seem, however, to be kindly fellows, and I mean to treat them well."

Such, indeed, had been the order of the authorities. Two soldiers were to keep watch over Warwick's person by day and by night, until further orders. If he should attempt to escape they were to shoot him down like a dog.

But even on those conditions Warwick was glad to be at large. He went straight from his prison to his mother's house. At his request the soldiers stood outside. That was a joyous meeting between mother and son. He told her all, and then, impatient to see his other friends, started for Granshaw.

CHAPTER XXIV.

SUSPENSE.

" Who fears to speak of Ninety-Eight ?
Who blushes at the name ?
When cowards mock the patriots' fate,
Who hangs his head for shame ? " — IRISH BALLAD.

IT was the month of May, 1798. Nature had donned her freshest, brightest garb. The skylark, as he soared aloft on fluttering wing, sang loud and cheerily. The thrush and blackbird piped in the groves and glens. The snowy lambs sported by their dams in the broad green meadows. The babbling brooks gave forth their music, and kissed and wantoned with the gaudy May flowers that blossomed by their margin. The fragrant violets peeped timidly from beneath the verdant hedgerows. The springing corn gave promise of a glorious harvest. The fleecy clouds floated like angels' drapery athwart the azure heavens. The sun rode high in his chariot, showering his golden smiles upon the gladdened earth, lighting up mountain and glen, hill and dale, castle and cottage, farmstead and hamlet. Earth seemed a very Paradise.

How fared it with old Ireland ?

How fared sweet County Down ?

Alas, the green fields seemed to smile in mockery. The harvest prospects cheered not the farmer's heart. The golden grain might bend before the autumn breeze unseen by him. The corn he sowed might ne'er be reaped by him. Nay, more, his own heart's blood might nourish the green roots ! He heeded not the duties of his farm. Each sun that rose, each sun that set, still found him on the watch.

For what ?

The call to arms.

Yes, it had come to that ! Rash and impetuous the people may have been, misguided and misled, goaded and forced to arms. The yoke of tyranny was upon them, and that yoke they must fling off !

In the South the people were in arms, and blood was spilled like water. Ay, and the Patriots were victorious, too, the redcoats scattering before the impetuous charges of the peasantry like chaff before the gale.

Then why did Down and Antrim sleep ?

Through treachery and cowardice !

But the treachery and cowardice were not of the people. They had their origin amongst the leaders !

And be it here remarked that the Government, fully informed of every movement of the people, having in their possession the leaders' names, the strength of the United Irishmen, and the quantities of arms, could at any moment have stamped out the agitation, suppressed the rebellion, and prevented a civil war with all its horrors.

Why did not the Government do so ?

Because that would not have suited its purpose. Blood must be shed ! Creed must war against creed ; faction against faction ; Ireland must be divided against herself, and then her chains would be rivetted the stronger.

These are facts recorded by history, and never attempted to be disproved.

While the South was in arms, the North was in comparative tranquility. This was contrary to general expectation, because it was here—especially in the Counties of Antrim and Down—that the United Irishmen's organisation first took root.

The 21st of May had been fixed for the rising. As the day approached, the Northern leaders lost courage and wavered. They became alienated from their friends in Dublin, and some of them were so base as to become informers ; others were arrested and thrown into prison.

An outbreak was daily, momently expected, and Government knew well that it would be one of terrible determination. The disaffection in the North was not the hasty ebullition of turbulent excitement ; it had progressed gradually, slowly but surely; it was the fixed and determined antipathy with which liberal feeling regarded established institutions. The rebellion in the South might be the evanescent outburst of a more fiery and impetuous people, but from Northern coolness, dogged determination and unflinching bravery, more real danger was to be anticipated. The conspiracy in the North had been a long-gathering storm, and the material of its violence had the more reason to be dreaded.

News travelled slowly in those days. There were no telegraphic wires encircling the earth's surface and winging tidings with the swiftness of the lightning's flash. The iron horse careered not over the length and breadth of the land. Newspapers were little larger than modern tracts. The couple published in Belfast were only issued twice a week, and they devoted more attention to " Court and Fashion," " Parliamentary and Foreign News," than they did to those affairs which concerned the people. Besides, these puny sheets were expensive, and people could not generally afford to buy them. Thus there was a dearth of news ; the wildest rumours were afloat concerning the doings in the South ; an enormous quantity of arms and ammunition were ready for the men of the North, concealed in every conceivable place, churches included. The men of the North were ready too, and awaited with angry impatience the call to arms But still the summons came not !

And now, even at this critical moment, had severities been discontinued, had efforts of a conciliatory nature been made, the flame, now flickering, might have been extinguished. But the reverse was the case. Promises were made but to be broken; proclamations which were commenced by offering an amnesty, merged into sanguinary denunciations, and ended by devoting whole towns to plunder and destruction by fire. The free quartering of the soldiery brought terror to Royalists and Insurgents alike. The army, thus quartered, abandoned themselves to all the brutal excesses of which a licentious soldiery could be capable, and, as the gallant Abercromie stated, they were formidable to all but the enemy. From the highest to the lowest, from the noblest mansion to the humblest hut, no one was safe or secure. Men, youths, ay, and women too, died under the lash ; many were strangled because they could not, or would not, make confessions ; hundreds were shot dead at their daily work, in their beds, in the bosoms of their families—all to amuse a wanton and brutal soldiery. Torture was inflicted without mercy and without regard to age, sex, or condition.

Many of the military atrocities in the South have been recorded in history, and they are beyond belief. The duties of the common hangman were discharged, in many cases, by the soldiers, some of whom acquired an unenviable notoriety for their cold-blooded brutality. Sergeant Dunn, of the King's County Militia, was a monster in human form, whose ferocious cruelty was perhaps without a parallel, even at the worst times of the French Revolution. Dunn would frequently have quite a number of executions on hand. On such occasions, he would quietly string up the first victim upon whom his choice fell, and the others were spectators of the dying man's agonies. When life was supposed to be extinct, Dunn would cut down the body, strip off the clothing, all save the shirt, and tie it up in a handkerchief. Then, removing the shirt from the yet warm body, he would coolly chop off the dead man's head and roll up the bloody trophy in the shirt. With the remaining victims, one by one he proceeded to deal in a similar fashion. When his work was done he was in the habit of selling the dead men's clothes, watches, rings etc., as " Rebel trophies." The heads rolled up in the shirts, he carried to his own house, where he fixed them on pikes. In the course of the evening he would proceed with these over his shoulders to the town-house, where he mounted the roof and secured them in an upright position to excite the horror of the people and the ribaldry of the soldiers.

Incredible as the foregoing may appear, it is nevertheless absolutely true ; and Sergeant Dunn had a rival in the person of Lieut. Hepenstal, concerning whom the late Sir Jonah Barrington has written. This fellow was six feet two inches high, broad in proportion and possessed enormous strength. He was known as " The Walking Gallows." He was an amateur executioner, and practised the profession in the following manner : When a prisoner, doomed to die, was brought to him, the lieutenant drew his fist and knocked him down. His garters he used for handcuffs, and then he pinioned him hand and foot, after which he advised him to pray for King George, adding that any time spent in praying for his own damned rebel soul would only be lost. During this exhortation the lieutenant would twist up his own silk cravat, slide it over the man's neck, secure it there by a double knot, and draw the ends over his shoulders. This done, an assistant lifted up the victim's heels, and Hepenstal, with a powerful chuck, would draw the man's head up as high as his own and trot about with him like a jolting cart-horse, until the poor creature was choked to death, when, giving him a parting chuck to make sure that his neck was broken, the brutal hangman would fling the dead body to his assistant to be stripped of its clothing.

When such deeds were done to men of wealth, position and influence, it may be imagined how the blood of the poor and humble flowed in torrents and unnoticed.

Little wonder that the Southern Patriots avenged these outrages with terrible ferocity !

Little marvel that the men of the North panted with eagerness to join in the fray !

CHAPTER XXV.

THE PITCH CAP.

" For ages rapine ruled the plains,
And slaughter raised his red right hand ;
And virgins shrieked and roof-trees blazed,
And desolation swept the land." — ANON.

THE month of June arrived, and the men of the North felt the crisis to be at hand.

It was at hand, and that crisis was doubtless accelerated by events some of which cannot be passed over in this narrative.

In a lonely hut, convenient to Newtownards, and quite close to what is now known as " The Gallows Hill," lived Jack Sloan, a poor blacksmith. Jack was unmarried ; a simple-minded, harmless creature, who lived alone, and was much of a recluse in his habits. He was an excellent tradesman, his charges were light, and he was—perhaps for that reason—rather a favourite with the farmers of the district.

In those days every man who worked at an anvil was suspected of manufacturing pike heads, and every country carpenter was suspected of making pike handles. These men required to exercise the strictest caution, and many of them were subjected not only to inconvenience by having their premises searched, but also to serious ill-treatment at the hands of the soldiery and yeomanry.

As far as can be ascertained, Jack Sloan refused to have any hand in the making of pikes. He was certainly not a United Irishman, and when he did converse with people upon the subject, he invariably urged upon them to have nothing to do with a rebellion, as no good would come of it. Thus he was, to all appearance, a loyal subject of the King, and one deserving to be exempt from the surveillance or interference of His Majesty's bloodhounds.

But the humblest man has his enemies, and Jack was no exception. Information was conveyed to Colonel Stapleton, at Newtownards, that Jack was never seen abroad ; that his anvil and bellows were at work every night, and that without a doubt large quantities of pike heads were being turned out at his forge. The name of the informer has never transpired—probably owing to what afterwards happened.

One day in the very beginning of June, 1798, as Jack worked away at his forge, he was astonished to see a party of soldiers surrounding the place. Dropping his hammer and a piece of iron which he had been fashioning into a gate bolt, the blacksmith stood gazing in speechless wonder.

" Ha ! " cried a soldier, " what's that ? "

As he spoke he picked up the unfinished bolt.

But he dropped it more quickly than he lifted it !

The iron was hot and burned his fingers severely.

" Damn you ! " he exclaimed, as he struck Jack with his musket, " you are making pikes ! "

Jack staggered under the blow, but, instantly recovering himself, he exclaimed—

" Afore God, gentlemen, sodgers, a em not makin' pikes ! "

" And what do you call *that* ? " said the first speaker, kicking the offending bit of iron across the floor of the smiddy.

" It's a boult for a man's gate ; it is indeed, sir," stammered the terrified creature.

" You're a rebel and a liar ; down on your knees !" said the soldier, who seemed to have command of the party.

Jack did as he was ordered.

" Now," continued the soldier, " say ' God bless his Majesty King George the Third ! ' "

With quivering lips, but with a loud voice, Jack repeated the words.

" And to hell with all United Irishmen and other rebels ! " said the soldier.

Jack made no response,

" Do you hear me ?" demanded the soldier.

" A dae, sir," said Jack, looking him steadily in the face.

" Then say what I desired you ! "

" A wull not, sir," said Jack, quietly but respectfully ; " a'll niver wush ony man tae gang tae hell ! "

" Then you'll soon be there yourself if you don't say as I told you ! " cried the brute, who, thus armed by the law and surrounded by armed men, bullied a harmless and defenceless man.

Jack was a hero ! The world never knew it. He did not even know it himself.

He was still upon his knees, and, clasping his hands, he turned his eyes upwards towards the blackened roof of the smiddy, while his lips moved as though in prayer.

" Open your mouth, sir, and do as I ordered you ! Curse the United Irishmen ! "

As the soldier spoke he drew his bayonet and thrust the point of it into Jack's mouth !

The flesh was cut, and blood trickled from the wound.

Jack rose to his feet amid the laughter and jeers of the soldiery.

" *A'll dee furst !* " he exclaimed. " A'm a loyal subject o' the King's—God bliss and preserve him—but a'm sorry he haes fellows like you aboot him."

This was going too far, but Jack did not know it.

The soldier who had already questioned him next ordered him to give up any pikes he had.

" A niver made a pike in my life," replied Jack, wiping the blood away that was flowing over his chin.

" You have pikes concealed somewhere ! " retorted the soldier.

" Na, no yin," said Jack.

" I'll make you find them ! " said his tormentor. " Come, lads, tie him to his own anvil, and give him a round hundred ! "

The soldiers gave a cheer, threw down their arms, and seized upon their victim.

" Try a pitch cap ! " cried one of the party.

" Have you got it ? " asked the leader.

" Half-a-dozen," was the reply, as the man handed one to his superior, who shouted—

" Here, boys, try this first ! We'll make him curse all the rebels from here to Wexford ! "

The pitch-cap torture was truly an infernal one. The invention of it is attributed to the North Cork Militia. At all events, they were the introducers of it in the County of Wexford. The caps were made either of coarse linen or strong brown paper, besmeared inside with pitch, and always kept ready for service. It was one of these that was about to be fitted upon the head of the unfortunate blacksmith.

Poor Jack looked on in silence, wondering what was going to happen .

One of the soldiers, seizing hold of the smiddy bellows, brightened up the fire. Another held the "cap" over the coals until the pitch had melted and attained boiling heat.

" Ready, boys ! " he shouted.

Jack was forced to sit down upon the floor, where he was held until the instrument of torture was fitted to his head.

His hair was short, a circumstance which proved unfortunate in two ways. The soldiers at once declared him to be a " croppy, " and the boiling pitch, penetrating to his scalp, burned him like molten lead.

With a yell of agony he dashed the human fiends aside, and sprang to his feet.

They had no wish to hold him now. That would have spoiled the sport.

The wretched creature rushed from the smiddy, followed by his tormentors, and darted off at headlong speed to a stream near hand, hoping to plunge therein his burning head. But he was not permitted. No sooner did his design become apparent than he was surrounded and knocked down. He rolled upon the ground in agony, his eyes starting from their sockets, and bloody foam issuing from his mouth.

" Where are the pikes ? " cried the leader.

" A hae nane ; no yin ! Afore God, a hae nane ! Oh, let me at the water ! " pleaded the suffering man.

" Where are the pikes ? " again demanded the soldier, and as he spoke he inflicted a deep bayonet wound on Jack's thigh.

For a moment the creature writhed in agony. Then, crawling to his knees, he pointed to a large beech tree growing some fifty yards off, and gasped—

" Dig at the fit o' that tree ! "

" Ha ! " exclaimed the soldier, " who was right ? Come, lads, follow me, and let him scratch his head till we return ! "

They scampered off to the tree pointed out. The soil encircling it was fresh and apparently untouched. But they plunged in their bayonets, and turned up the sod to a considerable depth.

" The old beggar has lied ! " they cried, " there's nothing here ! "

" All right," said the leader, " we'll give him the two fifties now."

The enraged soldiers returned with a rush to Jack. He was lying upon his face. The foremost of them seized him by the arms and swung him to his feet. As he did so, the others uttered a shout of dismay.

Their victim was dead !

He had sent them to the tree for a moment's respite, and in their absence he had terminated his agonies.

CHAPTER XXVI.

AN IMPORTANT ARREST.

" A horse ! a horse ! my kingdom for a horse !"

THE arrest and imprisonment of the Rev. William Steele Dickson are matters of history. The reverend gentleman did not dream of the interest taken in his movements by the Government and he went about his duties anticipating no interference. On the morning of the 29th May, 1798, he mounted his horse and started from the residence of the Rev. Mr. Sinclair, a Presbyterian clergyman of Newtownards where he had been on a visit, purposing spending the day with Major John Crawford, at Crawfordsburn, and to ride from thence to Belfast in the evening.

On his way to Crawfordsburn he met several gentlemen journeying to Belfast, who informed him that Major Crawford was not at home, and, on hearing this, he joined the party whom he had met and accompanied them to Belfast. On the next day he rode to Ballygowan House, the seat of Robert Rollo Reid, where he spent the afternoon and night. This he did with a view to be convenient to Saintfield, where he intended to buy a horse on the following day.

The 31st May was Saintfield fair day. Dickson attended the fair and paraded it for several hours looking for a suitable animal. This, however, he failed to find.

He mentioned his errand to some gentlemen whom he chanced to meet, and one of them said that he knew of a horse which was for sale and which would suit. The horse was the property of Captain George Sinclair, of Belfast. Dickson said he would be in Belfast upon the following day, and would like to see the horse there. On this being said, one of the gentlemen with whom he was conversing called out " Maginn !" Our former acquaintance, Nick Maginn, immediately came forward, and was instructed to request Captain Sinclair's servant to have the horse taken to Belfast next day.

Having so far settled his business, Dickson called at Elliott's Inn, Saintfield, to get some refreshment, but there was such an amount of hurry and confusion in the place that he could not, with comfort, obtain a morsel. He thereupon called with a gentleman friend, David Shaw, where the inner man was refreshed. That night he slept at Ballygowan, and next morning set out for Belfast. Here he found that Captain Sinclair was from home, and the horse could not be seen.

By appointment of Presbytery, Dickson was to preach at Ballee next day, and to administer the sacrament of the Lord's Supper on the day following. He reached Downpatrick at about eleven o'clock on the morning of 2nd June. Just as he was entering the Inn he was accosted by Captain Marshall, of the York Fencibles, who appeared excited and annoyed.

" Mr. Dickson, " he said, " I wish to speak with you. "

Dickson invited him inside, and having found an unoccupied room the two sat down.

" Now, Captain," said the clergyman, " I am at your service. "

" I have been in Portaferry in search of you, " said the Captain, " with a message from Colonel Stapleton. "

" And what was the nature of it ? " said Dickson.

" It appears that when you were at Mr. Sinclair's, in Newtownards, on Monday last, you said that a party of the Black Horse had gone over to the Insurgents. I am to enquire what grounds you had for making that assertion. "

" The matter is commonly reported, " replied Dickson, " and I merely spoke of it as a current item of news. It is generally believed to be true. "

" Will you kindly write that to Colonel Stapleton ? " said the captain.

" Certainly, " replied Dickson.

He at once procured writing materials, made out a full statement as requested, and added that should any further enquiry be deemed necessary he would be found at Ballee on the two following days, and in Portaferry at night ; that for some weeks afterwards he would be found at Ballynahinch from noon on Monday till the same hour on Saturday, and, on the intermediate time, in Portaferry, or the road between the two places.

This letter Dickson read to Captain Marshall, sealed it, put it in his hand, and saw it handed to a dragoon who was in waiting.

Dickson's object in going to Ballynahinch was to have the benefit of the Spa water, the use of which his doctor had recommended.

On the evening of the 5th June, while Dickson was sitting in his room, a servant informed him that a gentleman in the street wished to speak to him. On going out he met Captain Magenis and Lieutenant Lindsay, of the York Fencibles. At the request of Captain Magenis, Dickson walked out of town with him, when the Captain, after much hesitation and embarrassment, informed him that there had been a meeting of Yeomanry officers that day in Clough, and that he had received a letter from Colonel Lord Annesley, ordering his arrest.

" Do not be uneasy or alarmed," said Dickson, " I can bid defiance to malice itself, provided it be not supported by villainy. Where is your warrant for my arrest ? "

" I have only his lordship's letter, " replied Captain Magenis ; " *as you have a horse you may take a ride.* "

The gallant Captain wished his friend to escape the exposure of an arrest.

Dickson declined, and invited the captain and lieutenant to search his rooms. This they refused to do. He then suggested that they should place sentinels on the Inn, but this they also refused to do ; and it was only after considerable pressure that a sergeant was sent to the Inn to have an eye upon the clerical prisoner.

At noon, next day, a Colonel Bainbridge, from Lisburn, arrived in Ballynahinch, and ordered the removal of Dickson to Lisburn. Having given this order, he started for Montalto, to pay a visit to Lady Dowager Moira. Dickson, on learning this, sent a messenger after him to state that he was in delicate health, and to request that he might be permitted to ride or to travel in a chaise. The reply was as blunt as it was cruel.

" A chaise, and be damned ! Let him walk, or take a seat on the car which goes to town with the old guns ! "

Irritated with this harshness, Dickson determined to walk, which he did. They started about four o'clock in the afternoon, under a scorching sun, and reached Lisburn at eight in the evening.

Here he received more courteous treatment at the hands of General Goldie, who assured him of speedy liberation, and ordered a chaise to convey him to Belfast. But a disappointment awaited him on his arrival there. Instead of liberation, the order was—" Carry him to the black hole, and see that he is kept in safe custody ! "

CHAPTER XXVII.

FIRST BLOOD.

" Now with a shout that rends the air, ' Remember Orr !' they cry,
And like an avalanche dash on, to conquer or to die. "—T. C. S. CORRY.

THE arrest of Dickson occurred at a critical moment, the very eve of the outbreak.

The counties of Antrim and Down had resolved to work together and they would most certainly have been more than a match for the troops which garrisoned both. The 7th of June had been fixed for the rising, the respective duties were assigned, and everything was in readiness. But the arrest of Dickson left Down without a leader. Antrim was besought to wait until another had been chosen, but the men of Antrim, already weary of delay and deserted by Robert Simms, prepared to take the field, under the command of Henry Joy M'Cracken, of Belfast—a young man, well educated, accomplished and resolute.

The town of Antrim had been selected as the first object of Insurgent operation. It lay equidistant from the two great military stations—Belfast and Blaris Camp, and opened up communication with Derry and Donegal, from both of which counties extensive assistance was expected. The general rallying places for the County Antrim were the Roughfort and Donegore Hill, and thither, during the night of the 6th and morning of the 7th did the Insurgents march. The men were variously armed with guns, swords, pikes, pitchforks and scythes like Lochaber axes. They had also two small cannon—six-pounders—which had long lain concealed in the Templepatrick Dissenting Meeting House. They cut down a tree, and formed with it a trail for one of these, and having taken possession of a carriage belonging to Lord Templeton's agent, they mounted the gun upon its wheels.

Major Seddon was the military commandant at Antrim. Early on the morning of the 7th a messenger arrived from Colonel Nugent, who commanded the North-East District, bringing the startling intelligence that the people were in arms, and at any moment the town might be attacked.

The major was astounded and alarmed, but felt somewhat comforted when assured that he would be reinforced and enabled to repel the attack. By orders of General Nugent—who had been fully apprised of the movements of the Insurgents—the Second Light Brigade made a forced march from Blaris Camp on Antrim, while two hundred and fifty of the Monaghan Militia, a troop of the 22nd Light Dragoons, and the Belfast Yeomanry Cavalry, marched to support the garrison by the line of Carnmoney and Templepatrick.

What must have been the feelings of the residents of Antrim when, at the hour of nine o'clock, they saw the local garrison turn out, and heard the drums sounding the call to arms ! Within the town itself everything seemed as usual ; without the town, far as the eye could reach, no men bearing arms could be seen.

In response to the roll of the drum, the Yeomanry quickly mustered. The other male inhabitants were ordered to come out and fight in the defence of their town. Then, and not till then, was Major Seddon convinced that General Nugent's information was well founded. He discovered that the prominent United Irishmen had left town ere the dawn of day.

In answer to the summons, two hundred men turned out, but these could be supplied with only eighty stand of arms !

Ammunition was also scarce. Eight hundred rounds were borrowed from Major Seddon, and when this had been distributed, the Yeomanry had but twelve rounds a man, the Volunteers but five ! Troops shortly afterwards arrived, and the best possible arrangements were made for defence. The foot occupied a strong position in front of the castle gate ; the 22nd Light Dragoons, under Colonel Lumley, were covered by the walls surrounding the church, and here also the Blaris Moor men were mustered, while the cannon, planted near the centre of the town, commanded the wide and open street which extended between both.

And thus disposed, they waited for the Insurgent army !

At an ancient mound, called the Roughfort, the Irish flag was unfurled, when Henry Joy M'Cracken marshalled the first division of the Insurgent army. Here he was joined by the united troops of Templepatrick and Killead, many of whom had belonged to the old Volunteers, and were trained to the use of musket and artillery. Three other divisions, under different leaders, were instructed by M'Cracken as to their line of action.

M'Cracken formed his men into three divisions ; in front were the musketeers ; next came the pike men, and in the rere the gunners, with their two brass cannon.

" Forward, my lads ! " cried the leader, in a clear, commanding voice.

With firm and steady pace, and in the most perfect order, the march commenced. From the centre of each division waved bright green banners ; absolute silence was observed ; no sound but the heavy, measured tramp of the armed men, save now and then when the Marseillaise hymn was sung and its chorus swelled upon the morning air.

Antrim was in sight !

M'Cracken halted his men, and, turning round, surveyed them with a glance of pride and pleasure. His loose flowing locks were confined by the helmet which shaded his manly brow, and his eye beamed with the fire that animated his soul. His cheek was pale, for he had lain in a dungeon cell, but his heart was strong and knew no fear.

" Men of Ulster ! " he cried, " the hour has come for you to strike the first blow for Ireland and for liberty. Victory is certain ! Musketeers, let every bullet find its mark ! Pike men, stand firm in the shock of battle, and let your trusty blades, forged for you by true and trusty men, be a wall of steel upon which, if our foemen rush, they rush to death. Follow me, my noble fellows, wherever I may lead you, and let our war-cry be—' Remember Orr ! ' "

With a wild, ringing cheer the men advanced, and boldly marched into the town. They were met by a volley of case shot from the cannon, which told with slight effect upon their close column.

M'Cracken's men were not unnerved. With the coolness of veteran soldiers they continued the march over the bodies of the dead and dying. Another volley, yet they swerved not, waiting but their leader's order. It came at last.

" Fire ! " shouted M'Cracken.

There was a blinding flash, a roar of musketry, and the cavalry were forced to give way.

By this time a second division of the Insurgents had entered the town from an opposite direction and driven the infantry from the castle gate. A division of the pike men now fearlessly advanced upon the enemy's guns, intent upon carrying them. Repeated discharges of grape shot made havoc in their ranks, but with seeming indifference of death they rallied again and again. Repulsed at last, they gained possession of the church-yard, and, covered by the musketry, they had time to rally and form.

One of the Insurgent cannon to which reference has been made—that mounted on M'Vicker's carriage wheels—was disabled by its own recoil, observing which, the Light Dragoons, led by Colonel Lumley, made a charge, but he was received by a band of pike men and speedily repulsed. Maddened by defeat and the pain of a wound which he had received, Colonel Lumley launched some eighty of his men at the Insurgents who held the church-yard. It was a rash, if gallant deed ! In less than two minutes five officers, forty-seven rank and file, and forty horse were piked. The colonel fled with what was left him of his cavalry. Lord O'Neill attempted to follow, but his horse becoming restive, he was dragged off by a pikeman and slain.

M'Cracken, following up his success, drove the enemy from their guns, bore down rank after rank, fighting with the courage of a lion, and, in an hour from his entry, he was master of the town.

His victory was of short duration. A fatal blunder blasted his success and changed the fortunes of the day.

The United troops from the northern district of County Antrim had, by direction of their leader, M'Cracken, attacked Randalstown, where the military garrison, after a feeble resistance, surrendered. The troops then started, as arranged, to join M'Cracken at Antrim. As they neared the town they saw approaching them in the distance Colonel Lumley and his routed cavalry. The leader was a coward. Imagining that what he saw was the charge of victorious horsemen, and concluding that his arrival had been too long delayed, he gave the order tor retreat, and the men under his control fled in every direction ! Lumley's flying column, observing this, took courage and halted ; they were soon afterwards joined by reinforcements from Belfast and Blaris Moor, and, thus strengthened, they wheeled about to attack and retake the town.

A small corps of observation had, by direction of M'Cracken, followed the retreating military to watch their movements. These returned to Antrim in hot haste to report what they had seen, and their tiding caused a panic which rapidly extended.

It was a trying moment for M'Cracken. Everything that talent and courage could suggest was attempted to restore order and revive the flagging courage of his men, but all in vain. Driven almost to frenzy, he seized a pike, and placing himself in front, threatened with instant death the man who should dare to flinch from his colours. All was useless ; panic had seized upon the Insurgents, and they fled for their lives, actually bearing down in their wild flight the man who had proudly led them to victory. To many of them it was a fatal flight. They fell into the path of the advancing cavalry, who cut them down without mercy.

One division, called by M'Cracken " The Spartan Band," remained true and maintained its position. It was commanded by a man of high honour and great courage, named James Hope. This position commanded an easy entrance to the town, and a fierce but futile attack had been made upon it. A detachment of cavalry, which had debouched to the left, taking it to be in possession of the division to which they belonged, advanced at full gallop. To their alarm and surprise they were surrounded instantly, and, believing their slaughter to be inevitable, they, like brave men, awaited their fate in silence.

But Hope was generous as he was brave. " Go, " he said, " your numbers are too few for the sacrifice—join your comrades and tell them that the Union feels no triumph in the destruction of the defenceless and the weak."

The fate of the day had, however, been already decided, and Hope was at last compelled to abandon his post. His men made a last effort. Halting in the face of a victorious enemy, they presented a bold front ; they sustained the fire of musketry and cannon, and, when all hope of victory was over, they effected a retreat with order, planting their tattered colours on the heights of Donegore. Deserted by all but about a hundred men, M'Cracken resolved to march to Ballymena and join with those who held possession of that town. Having taken his post on the lofty Sleamish, he was surrounded by a force of four hundred disciplined troops. Still undaunted, he prepared for battle, when the British commander, Colonel Clavering, offered a full and perfect amnesty on their delivering up their four leaders, for whose bodies he further offered a reward of £400. M'Cracken's men spurned the proposal with indignation, and offered £400 for the body of Clavering living or dead. Clavering evidently feared to attack this bold remnant of the United Irishmen, and ultimately he threatened to destroy the surrounding country by fire and sword unless the Insurgent leader retired. Humanity compelled M'Cracken to leave his position.

It is needless to follow his movements further. He was soon afterwards captured, brought a prisoner to Belfast, tried by court-martial, and ordered for immediate execution. He died as only a brave man can.*

---

*The place of Henry Joy M'Cracken's execution was the Old Market-house, presented to the town by an ancestor of his own. The site is now occupied by the premises of Forster Green & Co., Ltd. The following account of M'Cracken's death is recorded by his sister:—

" The time allowed him had now expired ; about 5 p.m. he was ordered to the place of execution—the old Market-house—the ground of which had been given to the town by his great-great-grandfather. I took his arm, and together we walked to the fatal spot . . . . Harry begged I would go. Clasping my arms around him (I did not weep till then), I said I could bear anything but leaving him. Three times he kissed me, and entreated I would go, and fearing any further refusal would disturb the last moments of my dearest brother, I suffered myself to be led away. . . . I was told afterwards that poor Harry stood when I left him and watched me till I was out of sight ; that he then attempted to speak to the people, but that the noise of the trampling of the horses was so great that it was impossible he could be heard ; that he then resigned himself to his fate, and the multitude who were present at that moment uttered cries which seemed more like one loud and long continued shriek than the expression of grief or terror on

CHAPTER XXVIII.

HARRY MONRO.

" An Irish maid in heart and soul,
I love the dear old land ;
I honour those who in her cause
Lift voice, or pen, or hand. "

THE arrest of Dickson caused a remarkable sensation in the Ards district. It was immediately followed by the arrest of Colonel Bryson, of the Cottown, whose name had been given to the authorities as one who stood high among the leaders. Consternation and dismay prevailed upon all hands, and the question went from lip to lip—" Who next ? "

It was at this juncture, when the word had been given to take up arms, when Antrim was preparing to take the field, and when the hearts of Down looked on in silent expectation, that Harry Monro, of Lisburn, was, by general consent of those in authority, appointed General of the Patriot Army in Down.

Much has been said and written of Harry Monro. A nobler man never breathed. A braver man never took up arms in any cause. He was a linen merchant, residing in Lisburn, and was a regular buyer at the linen markets held in Ulster. In person he was remarkably handsome, and was exceedingly fond of dressing with neatness and taste. A portion of his back hair, in keeping with the fashion of the time, was worn very long, and tied with a black ribbon, hung over the collar of his coat. His conduct in private life has ever been spoken of as that of a perfect honour. Light-heartedness and love of fun were among his leading characteristics. Many instances of his bravery have been related—of his chivalry I shall speak hereafter. When

similar occasions. . . . Preparations were made for immediate burial. I could not bear to think that no member of his family should accompany his remains, so I set out to follow them to the grave. . . . I heard the first shovelful of earth that was thrown on the coffin, then I remember little else of what passed on the sad occasion. He was buried in the old churchyard, where St. George's Church now stands, and close to the corner of the School-house."

Amongst the numerous letters received by the author during the progress of this story in the columns of the " North Down Herald " is one from a County Down gentleman in which he says—" Henry Joy M'Cracken was buried in St. George's Churchyard, immediately behind Mr. Lindsay's warehouse. I was present with my grandfather and Miss M'Cracken (Harry's sister) in 1836 when they visited it, and their faces were not dry."

attending a linen market in Lurgan, on one occasion, an alarm of fire in the church of that town was raised. Harry Monro was chiefly instrumental in quenching the flames, and that, too, at the imminent risk of his life.

Monro was an Episcopalian, and warmly attached to his church, having been a churchwarden of Lisburn Cathedral. He had been a member of the Lisburn Volunteers, and when that body was suppressed by the Government he joined in the general indignation caused by the ingratitude of the State. He never contemplated taking up arms against the King's Army, and much less had he dreamed of leading the Insurgent host ; but, when the call was given, he considered his honour to be at stake, and he complied with the wishes of his brethren. It is told he took this final step after witnessing a public flogging in Lisburn.

The tidings spread rapidly, and caused universal rejoicing. Nowhere did the news cause more pleasure than at Granshaw. It was the hour of midnight on Friday, the 8th of June, and a party of tried and trusty friends were assembled at Betsy Gray's. Eliza Bryson was there with her brother, and Mary Stewart, though timid and faint-hearted, could not deny herself the pleasure of joining in the conference. The three girls sat by the fire ; the men, eight in number, sat around the table, discussing with animation the position of affairs and the events that were likely to happen.

" One thing must be done, " said David Bryson, " my father must be rescued. He is confined in the Newtownards Market-house, and, though I die in the effort, I shall attempt his rescue. "

" I am with you, my boy, " said George Gray.

" And I, and I, and I," exclaimed the others.

" An' a'll be at han', a'll warrant ye," said Mat M'Clenaghan, who formed one of the company.

" And now," said George Gray, " this is the last opportunity we may have of talking quietly together ; this is the last time we may all meet under this roof tree so let me give you a toast –

" Here's to old Ireland and General Monro ! "

All reserve was laid aside. True there were faithful sentinels posted outside to warn the inmates of the house should an enemy approach. But caution was abandoned, and the toast was drunk with cheers that made the rafters ring.

When the wild burst of enthusiasm had subsided, George Gray again spoke.

" You all know what the arrangements are," he said. " The hill of Ednavady, which looks down upon Ballynahinch, is to be our meeting place. From its lofty summit we can command a view of the country for miles around, and strong indeed must be the force that will drive us from that stronghold. From Bangor, Donaghadee, Newtownards, Crawfordsburn, Greyabbey, and other places, there will be a general march to-morrow. Once at Ednavady, our General will disclose his plans. But we have a duty to perform to-morrow. We must rescue Colonel Bryson and take him with us. That done, ' forward ' is the word, and every brave man will do his duty."

" Ay, and woman too ! " said a clear, sweet voice.

It was the voice of Betsy Gray !

" Yes, my good sister," said George, " yours will be a trying duty. When we are in the heat of conflict you will be here, enduring all the agony of suspense. But you can pray for our success. "

" No, George, I shall *not* be here ! " said the beautiful girl, as she stepped forward and placed her hand upon her brother's shoulder.

" Not here, Betsy ! And where will you be ? "

" At your side, wherever you may be, " she replied.

" Impossible ! " exclaimed George,

" No, not impossible, " said Betsy ; " I shall not be alone ; Eliza Bryson will be there too. "

" Oh, this is madness, " said George, while the others shook their heads in silence.

" Not a bit of it, George," said Eliza Bryson ; " where should we be but with our friends, to cheer them and to attend to their wants ? Oh, never mind, Betsy and I have it all arranged. "

Betsy darted into her bedroom, and returning, waved a sword round her head.

" See here ! " she exclaimed, as the blade flashed in the light of the candles, " I am prepared as well as the rest of you. Here is a weapon which will never betray me, and I shall show you all that I know how to wield it. "

George rose, and taking the sword from his sister's hand, surveyed it in speechless wonder.

It was a beautiful weapon, and of most exquisite workmanship. The handle was of green-stained ivory, with a slender chain attached ; the hilt was of silver, beautifully embossed, and bearing the letters N.R. The steel blade was so fine in quality and so highly tempered that it could be bent until point and hilt met.

" Betsy, where did you get this ? " enquired her brother.

" Ask Willie, " she replied, smiling, and looking archly towards her lover.

"Betsy, this must not be," said George ; " you must stay at home. "

" Never ! " said Betsy, drawing up her elegant figure to its full height. " This is not a time for even women to sit in idleness. George, where you go I go, though it be to slaughter and death ! "

" Bravo ! " cried Mat M'Clenaghan, who could no longer restrain himself.

And then it was that Betsy, with flashing eye and heaving breast, with her white hand grasping her gleaming sword, delivered an address that stirred the soul of every listener. Her words have been repeated by father to son, and have been immortalised by a poet who gives them thus :—

An Irish maid in heart and soul,
    I love the dear old land ;
I honour those who in her cause
    Lift voice, or pen, or hand.
And may I live to see her free
    From foreign lord and knave ;
But Heaven forbid I'd ever be
    The mother of a slave.

God bless the men who take their stand
    In Ireland's patriot host ;
I'd give the youth my heart and hand
    Who serves his country most ;
And if he fell, I'd rather lie
    Beside him in the grave,
Than wed a wealthy loon, and be
    The mother of a slave.

Thro' many a blood-red age of woe
    Our nation's heart has bled ;
But still she makes her tyrants know
    Her spirit is not dead.
God bless the men who for her sake
    Their blood and genius gave ;
God bless the mothers of those sons
    Who nursed no dastard slave !

Some on the scaffold place of doom
    For loving Ireland died ;
And others to the dungeon gloom,
    Are torn from our side ;
But God the Just who ne'er design'd
    His image for a slave,
Will give our country might and mind
    To raise the true and brave.

It was almost dawn when the party broke up. It had been a sleepless night ; a night of anxiety and suspense. Husbands and fathers kissed their wives and children, many of them for the last time on earth ; brothers and sisters and friends bade each other an affectionate farewell ; young men and old, eager to obey their leaders' orders, grasped their pikes and muskets and hied them away to the various mustering places. Ere the sun should again set, who could tell what might have happened !

CHAPTER XXIX.

THE GREYABBEY INSURGENTS.

" But stars oft gleam brightly when night's gloom is drearest,
To brighten the pilgrim upon his lone way,
So deeds of past heroes, whose fame we hold dearest,
Still flash through dark chaos a hallowing ray. " — CORRY.

ON the county road leading from Donaghadee to Greyabbey, and distant about one mile from the latter town, stands till this day the house in which the first branch of the United Irishmen's Society was organised in County Down. Grove Cottage, the name by which it is known, is a charming little house, picturesquely situated and kept in excellent order.

In the troublous times Grove Cottage was in the possession of Mrs. Sarah Byers, an aged widow, and her two sons, Alick and William.

On the night of Thursday, 7th June, 1798, there was a meeting in Grove Cottage of some half dozen of the Greyabbey Insurgents. Mrs. Byers was present at the consultation which was being held and the occasion was to her a trying one. Both her sons had resolved upon taking up arms, and a position of importance had been assigned to each. Their commissions had just been handed to them by David Bryson, Colonel Bryson's son.

" My father has been placed under arrest, " said young Bryson, " but be assured he will not be long a prisoner. We have laid our plans for his rescue, and he will march with us to the field of battle. "

Then, turning to Widow Byers, he said —

" Next time we meet, Mrs. Byers, there will be stirring stories to relate, and your sons will be crowned with glory. "

Mrs. Byers shook her head sadly and was silent.

" You are not despondent, surely ? " said Bryson.

"I am, " she answered. " I fear no good will come of this, and it is hard, indeed, to part from my two sons, neither of whom I may ever see again. "

" Never fear, mother, " said William Byers, " we will both come back to you hale and hearty. Cheer up ! "

" I cannot be cheerful, " said the widow ; " with one of you I would willingly part when your country calls, but to take both and leave me without a friend or protector—oh, it is too bad ! "

" It is, mother, " said Alick ; " one of us must remain. "

The mother's face brightened.

" Which will it be ? " she asked.

The two brothers looked at each other in silence.

" Will you draw cuts ? " enquired young Bryson.

Both nodded assent.

Bryson went outside, and returned a minute afterwards, holding in his closed hand two straws of unequal length. One end of each was visible.

" Now " he said, " the man who draws the longer straw remains at home."

The brothers drew simultaneously, and held the straws aloft, William had drawn the longer !

" So be it, mother," he said, " I'll stay with you. "

Thus it fell to the lot of Alick Byers to lead the Ballyboley contingent. So prevalent were informers in those days that almost every movement of the Insurgents was communicated to the authorities. The appointment of Alick Byers was that very night made known to Colonel Stapleton. William Byers, when in Newtownards on the following day, learned from a private source that his brother was about to be arrested. By a trusty friend he sent this information to Grove Cottage, and urged his brother to flight. Alick received the message, and told his mother not to be alarmed at anything which might happen. At the same time he resolved to await William's return before deciding how he should act. In the dusk of the evening he was standing upon the road just opposite Grove Cottage, watching for his brother's return. Suddenly a party of soldiers came in sight. They were too near to afford an opportunity of escape. The leader of the party shouted to Byers to stand, and this he did until the party was within a few yards of him, when he turned and ran into the house. The soldiers dashed after him. Some of them went into the kitchen and others into the parlour, but their man had disappeared. Suddenly the crash of breaking glass was heard, and, guided by the noise the pursuers rushed into the bedroom. The window had been knocked out of its frame, and the soldiers, concluding that he of whom they were in quest had made his escape in that direction, bolted after him, and scoured the country. But Byers had not escaped in the manner supposed. With remarkable presence of mind he had sent a chair flying through the window, while he himself crept under the bed where he lay until the soldiers were out of hearing.*

On the morning of Saturday, 9th of June, the Cottown and Granshaw men, armed with pikes, guns and other weapons, marched for Newtownards, determined to effect the rescue of Colonel Bryson. David Bryson, the Colonel's son, had gone into Newtownards during the night for the purpose of ascertaining the exact position of affairs. He spent several hours with a friend who resided in Francis Street. While here he learned that at an early hour on Saturday, Colonel Stapleton, with nearly the entire force under his command, would march for Saintfield, where a large number of Insurgents had assembled.

This was cheering news for young Bryson, who knew well that the chances of a rescue were small in the face of the troops quartered at Newtownards and ready at any moment to respond to a call to arms.

Mounting his horse, he rode to Grove Cottage, where he found his trusty friend, Alick Byers, and informed him of how matters stood. It was arranged that during the night the men of Ballyboley, Greyabbey, and neighbourhood should arm themselves and march for Newtownards, where, next morning, they, with the contingents from Cottown and Granshaw, should attack the Market house and rescue Colonel Bryson. Having rested for a brief period, young Bryson returned to Newtownards, without interference, and spent the remainder of the night there.

* Alick Byers led his men to the battle of Ballynahinch and fell in the fight. His decomposed body was afterwards identified by his linen upon which his name was embroidered. Singular to relate, a splendid grey horse, upon which he had ridden to the battle, was found grazing in a meadow close to Ednavady, many weeks after the fight and was taken back to the old homestead. Some time after the battle of Ballynahinch William Byers was arrested and marched from Grove Cottage to Newtownards in charge of a military escort. Nothing could be proved against him, however, and he was released. Suspicion was strong against him, and orders were given to burn Grove Cottage to the ground. Montgomery, of Rosemount, interfered, and upon his representations the cruel order was cancelled.

The morning dawned, and during its early hours the inhabitants of Newtownards witnessed a stirring scene. A detachment of the York Fencible Regiment, accompanied by the Newtownards and Comber Yeomanry, Cavalry and Infantry, numbering altogether close upon a thousand men, were marshalled in the Market Square. Their bayonets and shining musket barrels gleamed in the light of the summer sun, and the men were as gay as though bent upon a holiday march. Colonel Stapleton, mounted upon a spirited horse, surveyed his men with a look of pride.

Amongst the officers were Captain Chetwynd, Lieutenant Unit, and Ensign Sparks. The Newtownards and Comber Yeomen were led by Captains Houghton and Cleland. The Rev. Mr. Mortimer rector of Comber, accompanied the Yeomen of that town.

The departure of the troops was witnessed by crowds, but ere the military had proceeded many hundred yards along the route of march the streets were almost deserted, the people retiring to their houses, for safety, or to make preparation for joining in the approaching conflict.

A small armed force had been left in charge of the town, and the men composing it were posted in the Market-house.

No sooner had Colonel Stapleton and his army marched from Newtownards than David Bryson mounted his horse and galloped off to join his friends from Granshaw and Cottown. He met them about a mile from the town, and a halt was made for consultation.

The Insurgents were led by George Gray and Willie Boal, who, it was well known, were to have assigned to them positions of importance on reaching Ballynahinch. The two young men were dressed in green jackets turned up with yellow, white vests, buckskin breeches, and half boots, while their hats were ornamented with green cockades. The uniform suited them to perfection.

Eliza Bryson, seated on a fine horse, rode in front. She was dressed in green silk and wore a white feather in her hat. Betsy Gray had remained behind. Her brother George had peremptorily forbidden her to join them ; her entreaties and tears were of no avail with him, and at last she consented to stop at home. But in her heart she resolved not to be far behind, and to join her friends at Ednavady ere the first shot would be fired upon an advancing foe.

The consultation held by David Bryson with his friends, George Gray and Willie Boal, did not occupy many minutes, and at its close George briefly addressed his followers, telling them of the work that lay before them, and how it was to be accomplished. The object in view was simply the rescue of Colonel Bryson and any other prisoners who might be with him. Bloodshed was to be avoided if possible, and no man was to use arms unless to defend his life.

At this juncture a man was seen running rapidly towards them from the direction of Newtownards. As he ran he waved a green handkerchief.

He was soon recognised as a scout from Greyabbey, and his news was cheering. Alick Byers and his men were awaiting them close to Greenwell Street.

With a wild " hurrah " the march was resumed. Half an hour later they met their brother patriots at George's Street, and hearty greetings were exchanged. The united forces were addressed by George Gray, who briefly disclosed his plans. Strict silence was enjoined and strictly observed. The march down Frances Street was at a quick and steady pace. From almost every window the pale faces of terror-stricken watchers could be seen. Soon the rere of the Market-house was reached, and the men filed round the corner into the square. As they did so the single sentry on guard stood for a moment paralysed, then uttered a shout and fired off his musket in the air. In an instant the upper windows of the building were thrown open, and a perfect babel of confused voices, mingled with the clash of arms, was heard.

" Keep close, my men ! " shouted Gray, making a dash for the door, followed by his supporters. Entrance was gained in less than a minute, and the men poured in. At this instant a volley of musketry was discharged by the soldiers from the windows, but their aim, whether wilfully or through nervousness, was faulty. Several were wounded, and one man was killed. The next moment the Insurgents came rushing from the building accompanied by Colonel Bryson and several other prisoners, who, having heard the alarm and guessed rightly its meaning, boldly attempted an escape, and actually fell into the arms of their rescuers.

The voice of George Gray was heard above the din shouting his orders, and, in less time than is required to relate the circumstances, the whole force had regained Frances Street and re-formed into marching order.

The military made no attempt to follow.

A halt was made near the head of Frances Street, and a supply of liquor having been procured, it was distributed among the men, who, with hearty cheers, drank the health of Colonel Bryson and success to their cause. They then struck out upon the Greyabbey road and resumed their march.

The Londonderry family had sailed for Liverpool on the previous night. The Granshaw men learned this fact from the Greyabbey and Ballyboley men, and it was determined to pay a visit to Mount-stewart house and grounds. A few men servants, who had been left in charge, fled on the approach of the Insurgents, who gambolled about the grounds like a pack of merry schoolboys. No attempt was made to injure the house or premises, but a visit was made to the well-stocked dairy, from which Eliza Bryson freely distributed milk and cream to the thirsty men.

A good deal of chaff was indulged in as to who should be the ultimate proprietor of the handsome house and grounds, but the fun was interrupted by the sound of drums. The look-out reported the approach of further contingents of the Insurgent army, and George Gray, Willie Boal, Colonel Bryson and Alick Byers hastened away their men to join the others.

* * * * * * * * * * *

Down was in arms by the morning of Sunday, the 10th of June.

The men who had been appointed to communicate the signal in the various towns, villages, and districts, and who were called " warners, " did their duty promptly and well, so that the rising was general and all but simultaneous.

There were many scenes and instances of a remarkable character. Thousands of persons, too timid to take up arms on either side, fled to Belfast for refuge, leaving behind them nearly all their worldly goods.

In numerous places efforts were made to induce loyally disposed persons to join in the rising, but these efforts met with little success. One remarkable instance is worthy of mention. Stewart Bell, of Ballywooley, Crawfordsburn, was a lieutenant in the Bangor Yeomanry, and a man of unswerving loyalty. Publicly and privately he had frequently remonstrated with the people against joining in the rebellion, and on this account his life and property were threatened with destruction. On the morning of Sunday, the 10th June, at about five o'clock, several men galloped up to the house on horseback, aroused the inmates, and called upon Bell at the peril of his life to join the Insurgents. As soon as they had left, Bell went to Crawford and consulted with him. He was advised by this gentleman to get a pass and cross to Greenock. On his way back he fell in with bands of the Insurgents going towards Bangor, and in consequence of their threats he was compelled to accompany them thither. At Bangor he found a large body of men awaiting the arrival of Hugh M'Cullough, who was to lead them to Newtownards. In vain Bell sought for an opportunity to escape from his unpleasant position. He was compelled to go with the people to Conlig, where, after a halt, a start was made for Comber. When about half way to Comber news was received that Colonel Nugent, with a large force, was marching from Belfast to meet them. Alarmed by these tidings, the Insurgents crossed by the fields to Scrabo mountain, and planted their standards there. At this point Bell managed to get free from his company. He was, however, afterwards arrested and thrown into Downpatrick jail. When his trial came on, he owed his life to the evidence of one of his servants. Similar cases could be cited, but I must hasten to describe the terrible events which transpired from the 9th to the 13th of June.

CHAPTER XXX.

A FEARFUL FATE.

" No hope of help ! No chance of flight !
Better to die in open fight !"—OLD BALLAD.

ONE mile from Saintfield and about three hundred yards off the Lisburn Road stood the house occupied by Hugh M'Kee and his family. It was new, substantially built of blue stone, slated, two storeys high, with windows in front and gable, but none in the rere. The foundation was partly cut out of the face of a hill.

M'Kee was a comfortable farmer ; he and his family had received numerous prizes from the Linen Board for their success in cultivating flax and spinning yarn. Several old spinning-wheels which they obtained as prizes are still to be seen in the neighbourhood, given by them as presents to their relatives.

The household consisted of M'Kee, his wife, five sons—the youngest sixteen years of age—three daughters, grown-up women—as daring as the father and sons, and afraid of nothing ; the whole family large, stout and robust, so much so that they were generally described by their neighbours as " a lot o' big, fat, coorse fowk. " There was also in the house a blind girl, aged about thirteen, who was a relative, and a servant named John Boles.

M'Kee and his family were most unpopular. The father had made himself obnoxious by persecuting United Irishmen, and by his offensive ultra-loyalty. The family were in the habit of going out at night, challenging every one they met on the road, and firing shots to the terror and indignation of people who passed their house. So great was the fear they thus inspired that many persons were in the habit of making a detour through the fields. One night a United Irishman, named Samuel Adams, was shot through the arm and side. Nelly M'Kee, a daughter of Hugh, seized a hatchet and attempted to hack off the man's head, remarking that " deid men tell nae tales ! " Two Scotch soldiers who were in the house at the time prevented the perpetration of the deed.

When Nicholas Price, of Saintfield House, brother-in-law to Lord Camden, tried to raise a corps of Yeomanry, the M'Kees were the only parties who could be induced to join. M'Kee evidently dreaded the resentment which his conduct was calculated to bring about, and he applied to the authorities for protection. A guard of two or three soldiers was frequently kept in the house, but previous to the outbreak of the rebellion this guard was withdrawn. He had a liberal supply of arms and ammunition from Dublin Castle, and he and his family were well trained to the use of weapons of warfare.

M'Kee's name and doings were familiar to the immense army of United Irishmen that on the morning of Saturday, 9th of June, '98, was under march to Ballynahinch. A council was held by the leaders, at which it was resolved to put an end to the insults of the M'Kees, and what was even more important, to seize the large store of arms and ammunition which they held. A party was detached for the purpose, headed by John Breeze, of Killinchy. When the object of the attack became known, the entire of the insurgent army in Saintfield turned out to witness the affair.

On that memorable morning M'Kee was apprised by a friendly neighbour that an armed host was under march to his house, and that unless he consented to join the insurgents he might expect to be strung up to the nearest tree.

" Then a'll niver join them, " said M'Kee, " an' a'll sell my life dearly."

He kept his word !

M'Kee entered his house, summoned his family, and told them what he had heard. No surprise was expressed ; the tidings had been long expected, and with the utmost coolness and deliberation the M'Kees began to barricade the doors and windows. A daughter of the yeoman kept watch from an upper window in the gable of the house, which commanded a view of the road along which the Insurgents were expected to approach. As she kept watch her father and brothers loaded their guns, collected their ammunition and arranged their course of action. If attacked, they were to fire from the windows ; the women were to load the weapons, the men to fire with sure aim, and all declared that they would die rather than surrender.

M'Kee's daughter kept watch at her little window. Every now and then from the kitchen below came the query—

" Dae ye see ocht ? "

And in a voice that quavered not was sent the answer—

" Na, naethin' yit."

All was in readiness. The defences of the little citadel had been made as complete as possible, and the time seemed so long that a ray of hope struggled for entrance into the father's heart—a hope that the alarm had been a false one.

But that hope was strangled in its birth. From the upper room came the message, conveyed in a suppressed shriek—

" Da, a see sumthin' noo !"

M'Kee sprang to the window. His sight was not so keen as that of his daughter, and he saw only what looked like a cloud on the distant horizon.

It was the cloud of dust raised by the feet of ten thousand men !

Then there were flashes, like rays of sunlight bursting from the cloud.

It was the gleaming of the polished pike heads in the morning sun !

" Cum awa frae the windey, dear, " said M'Kee, taking his daughter by the arm. " Gang wi' the ithers, an' dinnae be yin bit feered. "

Ere long the distant shouts of the Insurgents could be plainly heard.

To M'Kee and his family it was a sound of terror. It drove the blood from their cheeks and quickened their feverish pulses.

It was the hour of noon, and the sun shone with a fierce brilliancy. There had been a long season of drought ; the grass was scorched, and the dust lay piled upon the roadways. Parched with thirst, wearied by marching, and panting for vengeance, the mass of men moved onward. They crowded on the rocks and hills round about, pikemen with shouldered pikes in the rere, and the musketeers in front to watch the attack of John Breeze and his men.

They had not long to wait !

To the inmates of the doomed dwelling every minute seemed an age. From without there came the confused hum of many voices but no words were audible.

Suddenly a hand was laid upon the latch. But the door was bolted and barred, and heavy articles of furniture were piled against it from within.

" Open the door ! " cried a voice, and immediately a shower of blows was rained upon it.

" What do you want ? " cried M'Kee from within.

" We want you and your sons to join the Patriot Army, " was the reply.

" It's what we'll niver dae ! " was M'Kee's firm response.

There was a momentary silence without. The crowd awaited the result of the parley between their leader and M'Kee.

That result was quickly communicated. No sooner was it made known than there arose a shout so wild, so fearful, that froze the blood in the veins of the unfortunate informer and his family.

" Hang the informers ! " " Burn the house over their heads ! " " Teer doon the wa's an' let us at them ! " yelled the crowd, as it surged and swayed around the dwelling.

" Ready ! " whispered M'Kee to his sons, as he threw his musket to his shoulder and pointed to a window.

His example was followed by his sons.

There was no need to take aim. The veriest novice in the use of fire-arms could not fail to strike some one in that dense mass of human beings.

" Fire ! "

There was a crash of musketry and breaking glass ; there were shouts of fury and the shrieks of wounded men.

Breeze himself received a bullet in the leg, and howled in agony.

The volley from the house was promptly replied to by one from without, but no one was injured by it.

" Now ! " cried M'Kee, " it's life or daith ; load, lasses, an' we'll fire. "

The women never quailed. Mother and daughters loaded the muskets ; father and sons stood ready to fire.

It was slow work in those days loading the heavy guns, fixing the priming, looking to the flints and adjusting the locks. Ere a second volley could be fired the space in front of the house was cleared of men, and those who had fallen were dragged away.

There was a hurried consultation ; brief and decisive.

" Burn them ! "

Such was the sentence, and it was speedily carried into effect.

The attacking party made a detour to the hill at the back of the house. There were no windows there, and they were safe from the musketry of the M'Kees. Some of the men were sent to the house of a man named William Dodd for a ladder, which they obtained. On their way back they met two young men, William Shaw and William M'Caw, whom they compelled to carry the ladder. The young men, hearing what was about to be done, threw down the ladder and refused to carry it to M'Kee's house.† Some of the others took up the ladder, and on reaching the house placed it against the back wall. One of the men, by name Charles Young, climbed to the roof and removed a few slates. The aperture thus made displayed a pile of flax. The fellow laughed at the discovery, and shouted for a light. Some one handed him a blazing wisp of straw, and this he flung on the flax inside. The next instant the huge dry mass was in flames !

The hapless creatures within soon discovered the appalling fate in store for them. Driven to madness by the near approach of a death so horrible, and by the impossibility of escape, the imprisoned men tore away the barriers which they had put up against the windows and fired into the crowd in front. Every shot told, but they were few and far between. The women, who had realised the true state of affairs, gathered round their male relatives, clinging to them wildly and crying to God for mercy. Shots were fired into the house from all sides, and the frantic inmates huddled together out of the way of

† Charles Young, who placed the ladder against the house, turned King's evidence, and received a pension for life. James Gardner, another chief actor in the burning, also turned King's evidence, and received a pension. He was not personally acquainted with Breeze, but went to his house in Killinchy under the pretext of buying wheat, and by that means was able to identify him as the man who was at M'Kee's burning. On this testimony Breeze was hanged. The two young men, William M'Caw and William Shaw, who were forced to carry the ladder a short way, were also hanged by the evidence of these scoundrels. It was also chiefly on their evidence that the whole eleven persons were hanged—one for each individual burned; and it is confidently believed that all, except Breeze were entirely innocent. John Boles made the twelfth victim.

the bullets. But they could not long escape the flames. The dried flax and wooden beams burned like match-wood, and the fierce heat scorched the skin and singed the hair of the doomed ones.

In this fearful hour the women displayed remarkable courage and presence of mind. They carried crocks of cream from the milk-room, and, lifting the cream in handfuls, anointed the burns caused by the blazing pieces of wood and flax which fell upon them, and threw on each other the milk, to damp their clothes and relieve their sufferings.

John Boles, the servant, threw down his gun with a scream of agony as a mass of burning flax struck his head and face.

" Mester ! " he cried, " A can stan' it nae langer. Ony daith wud be better nor this. Apen the daur an' let us mak a dash oot an' fecht fur our lives ! "

M'Kee instantly agreed, and made a dash for the door ; but the women pulled him back by sheer force, and declared that they would all die together.

" Then A'll gang mysel' ! " shouted Boles. As he spoke he dashed through one of the shattered windows, and started to run for dear life.

The race was short. He was impaled upon a pike and fell mortally wounded.*

A minute later the ammunition exploded in the house with a noise like the discharge of cannon ; the roof fell in with a sickening crash, burying beneath its smouldering timbers the entire family, and stifling their piteous and heartrending screams.

The spectators fled in terror from the scene of this deed of horror. Next day a party of soldiers when digging among the burned ruins found numerous guns and pistols at the windows, with the stocks burned away. They also came upon a charred mass that looked " like a load of black sods " piled in a corner. Nothing in that mass could be distinguished as human, but a quantity of calcined bones proclaimed it to be the remains of the ill-fated M'Kee family. These remains were buried in the garden opposite the house, and the body of Boles was placed along with them a few days later. The unmarked grave is shown to this day.

* Singular to relate, Boles was left for dead, and was afterwards picked up by some friendly neighbour. He lived for two days, and told the facts above narrated.

CHAPTER XXXI.

THE BATTLE OF SAINTFIELD.

" It is, it is the cannon's opening roar ! "—BYRON.

THAT clumsy and bungling would-be historian, Sir Richard Musgrave, attempted very shortly after the '98 rising to write an account of the Battle of Saintfield. He succeeded to his own satisfaction possibly, but his version has generally been pronounced to be the reverse of accurate. He states, for instance, that Colonel Stapleton having attacked the Insurgents, " repulsed and killed 350 of them. " This should mean that 350 rebels were repulsed and afterwards killed. In the next paragraph he states that the rebels retreated towards Newtownards ; but further on he records the fact—and fact it was—that " a numerous body of rebels kept possession of Saintfield till Monday, 11th June, " the battle having been fought on the 9th. That is his sole account of the affair. My readers shall know more than that.

Harry Monro, of Lisburn, accompanied by a considerable body of men, joined Dr. Jackson, of Newtownards, and those whom he led, shortly after the destruction of M'Kee and his family. Monro, having been unanimously elected as commander-in-chief, he assumed the position assigned to him, and having been apprised of the fact that Colonel Stapleton was on the march towards Saintfield, he made preparations for the first brush with the military.

The men under his command were a mixed and varied multitude. Uniform they had none, but most of them presented a good appearance, being dressed in the best clothes which they possessed. Nearly every one wore a rosette or knot of green ribbon, and most of them had in their button-holes or hats sprigs of green. The majority carried pikes—deadly instruments of warfare at close quarters. These pikes had wooden shafts, about seven feet long, with sharpened heads of iron of different forms, ten or twelve inches in length ; some of these heads consisted of one piece, others had hooks attached to the blades, for the purpose of cutting the bridles of their opponents' horses. Not a few of the men were armed with swords, some carried guns, others merely pitchforks.

Saintfield is a small town about fifteen miles from Belfast, on the road to Downpatrick. Its Irish name, Tonaghneeve, signifies " the field of the saint. " A writer in 1774 stated that it had, not many years ago, been made a town, " by the care and industry of General Price, who began to improve here, opened and made the roads passable from Belfast to Down through it, encouraged linen manufacturers and other tradesmen to settle here, had a barrack fixed for a troop of horse, and promoted the repair of a ruinous, now decent parish church, to which he gave plate and other ornaments. " It is now a clean, neat little town, surrounded by a well-cultivated and populous country, undulating in hill and dale. But the hills are not so high as to forbid cultivation ; and in the old times the roads ran straight over their highest points, according to the ancient customs in other parts of Ireland, where the people had not learned the art of evading a difficulty by going round it. This change of roads has altered the aspect of many a locality, so that an old plan of the battle-field would show roads, houses, and other objects which modern improvement has completely obliterated. For example, only a small portion of the high road through the defile in which Colonel Stapleton and his men were entrapped now exists, like a lane running through some fields. But the grand features of the country, the hills and the valleys, still remain—the hills being despoiled of the woods with which they were then crowned, and the small river flows in its old channel through the scene of the battle.

The Insurgents had occupied the town of Saintfield, which was altogether friendly, when news came of the intended march of the troops to attack them. Partly to save the town, and partly as a stratagem, they took possession of a wood about a quarter of a mile on the Belfast road, where they lay in ambush completely concealed. It was an excellent position, affording a safe means of retreat, and ending at one side in a bog that prevented their being flanked by the enemy. In front of the wood there was some open ground, and between this ground and the road there was a thick hedge, behind which a number of the Patriots lay concealed, and through which they opened a murderous fire on the cavalry, driving them back on the infantry, and throwing them into confusion. There was also a wood on the lower side of the road, but this was not occupied by the Patriots at first, although in the course of the fight a portion of them subsequently availed themselves of its shelter. When the Royal troops advanced on the Comber road as far as Shepherd's house, which is still standing, Colonel Stapleton ordered a halt, suspecting that matters were not altogether right in front. One of three captives, John Lackey, Alexander Fitzsimmons and John Frame, whom he had seized on his march, advised him to take the whole force up the grove or wood, as it would be dangerous to pass between the high hedges and woods into the town. The Rev. James Clewlew, vicar of Saintfield, and the Rev. John Cleland then volunteered to reconnoitre. They rode rapidly as far as the bridge, and on their return reported that there was no enemy to be seen. It was believed that the main body of the Patriots was still in the village, as some of them were seen on the Killinchy road, and a number of spectators on the Windmill Hill. Colonel Stapleton, however, ordered the light company to advance. They marched along the top of the hill into Shepherd's field till they came in front of a high close hedge, where they received a heavy fire of musketry, which they returned. A line of pikemen then rushed out on the soldiers, and both parties, mingled together, went fighting down the hill to the road. The pikemen here encountered the main body. A desperate hand-to-hand struggle ensued in the narrow pass. Cavalry and infantry were crushed together in a confused mass, and in a short time the Royalists were driven back by overwhelming numbers to Shepherd's house. The pikemen then entered Doran's wood at the lower side of the road. Both parties now opened a general fire, which after a time died away. A sort of truce was hastily agreed upon, and Colonel Stapleton was permitted to take away his wounded men, a few of whom were left and taken care of in Shepherd's house. After remaining a few hours near the field of battle without attempting to enter the town, the Royal troops retreated to Comber, and were lodged during the night in one of the Presbyterian meeting-houses, proceeding next morning to Belfast.

The affair happened about six o'clock on Saturday afternoon and was over in less than an hour. On Sunday morning fifty-six dead bodies of the military and thirty-six of the country people were counted on the field. It was stated that many more of the latter were killed, but their relatives carried them away during the night. They appear to have had no general. Two men, named Fraizer and M'Kinstry, led the charge of pikemen down the hill. So fierce was their onset at the place where they burst through the hedge, that soldiers and pikemen were found lying together in rows. M'Kinstry was killed. Captain Unit, Lieutenant Chetwynd, and Ensign Sparks were also among the dead. The Royal forces were estimated at 900 or 1,000 men—800 York Fencibles and about 150 Yeomen. The Patriots are supposed to have numbered several thousand. The battle extended from the ambuscade to Shepherd's house ; and, by the troops not immediately engaged in the hand-to-hand fight, a simultaneous fire was kept up from the road and the field on the hill, directed towards the ambuscade, the troops continuing to fire during their retreat. Monro was not present on this occasion. There is no doubt that whoever had the chief command, Richard Fraizer was the leading spirit of that day.

The Rev. Mortimer, of Comber, was killed by one of the first shots. Every bullet has its billet, and that one true to its aim brought the reverend gentleman to the dust.

The United men entered Saintfield and remained in undisputed possession of the town.

Thus the first engagement resulted in the defeat of the military. The newspapers of the period speak of the Comber Yeomanry as having displayed much gallantry. Captain Chetwynd received nine pike wounds, at length he was struck by two musket balls, which ended his life.

An incident occurred in Comber which is worth relating. An officer, while on the march from Newtownards, halted his men at a public-house in Comber and ordered the proprietor to supply them with drink.

The publican may have been a loyal man, or he may have been the reverse, at all events he considered that he might have some difficulty in recovering payment for his liquor, and therefore he enquired—

" An' who'll pye me ? "

" Serve the liquor and ask no questions, " said the officer.

" A wull whun ye gie me the money, " was the dogged reply.

The officer had the publican instantly seized and held fast by a couple of men, whilst he sent half a dozen of the others into the shop with orders to carry out to his company as much liquor as they required. No second order was required. The men drank freely, after which they turned on every tap in the bar, so that the liquor might escape. The officer then ordered the release of the publican, and, as he rode off, he shook his sword in the poor man's face, and swore that on his return from Saintfield he would burn his house to the ground.

The officer fell, and some days afterwards his dead body was borne through Comber in a cart. By a singular coincidence, the men in charge of the body stopped at the same public-house for refreshment. The publican went out to examine the body, and instantly recognised his troublesome customer. Taking the dead man's hand, he exclaimed, chuckling inwardly at his little joke—

" An' what wae ir ye the day ? Man, but a'm gled tae see ye sae quate by what ye wur the tither day ! "

An eye-witness relates a revolting sequel to the battle of Saintfield, to the following effect:—Every one of the fifty-six dead bodies left by the Royalists on the scene of the conflict was stripped naked by the country people—not an article of clothing was left on any of them ; even the Reverend Mortimer was found sitting against a gate in the same state of perfect nudity. Two boys were seen fighting over the body of a dragoon for his uniform. A grave was dug in a mud bank in the river, and into it the bodies were laid indiscriminately, having been brought down in cart loads. Upon the little island thus formed the grass grows rich and green, and the clear stream runs murmuring by, as if no such tragedies could have been prepetrated in the midst of scenery suggesting nothing but rural happiness, quietness, and perfect peace, which indeed are now the characteristics of the place. This island of the dead is still known as " Jork Island. " Many of the Insurgents were buried in the adjoining Presbyterian graveyard, suitable tombstones marking their graves.

CHAPTER XXXII.

EDNAVADY.

" By easy steps I regularly rise,
Where Ednavady's top salutes the skies,
And view with pleasure all the distant fields,
The nobler scenes which fair Montalto yields,
Where once a hawthorn bush and bramble grew,
A turf, and rocks unpleasing to the view,
Now sprouting groves disclose a smiling green,
And blushing flowers, intruding, glance between ;
Here the sublime of nature wakes surprise ;
Where there the gentle charms attract the eyes. "

THE town of Ballynahinch, in the County of Down, lies about twelve Irish miles from Belfast. It has long been a favourite resort of those in search of health, and is widely celebrated for its famous spas, which have occupied a high place in public estimation for upwards of a century.

The parish name of Ballynahinch is Magheradroll, which signifies " The Field of Difficulties. " A hundred years ago the place was most difficult of approach, and writers of those days speak of the country surrounding it as being extremely coarse, full of rocks and hills, rendering access to it troublesome and unpleasant, and drawing bitter complaints from travellers who could only hobble through the broken and narrow causeways.

All that, however, is now changed. Good roads have been made, and travellers from Belfast can accomplish the journey with ease by means of the County Down Railway. The distance by rail is twenty-one miles, and the railway is one of the smoothest in the kingdom. Harris, in his history of County Down, speaks of Ballynahinch as lying in the midst of the great roads leading from Lurgan, Lisburn, Dromore, and Hillsborough to Downpatrick. It was founded after the wars of 1641, by Sir George Rawdon, Baronet, an ancestor of the Marquis of Hastings, in the possession of which family it remained till the early part of the last century. The family of Hastings is of great antiquity, as is shewn by the title deed of their estate, in which the following fines appear : –

" I, William King, the third year of my reign,
Give to Paulyn Royden, Hope and Hopetowne,
With all the Landes, both up and down,
From Heaven to Yearth, from Yearth to Hel,
For thee and thine, there to dwel,
As truly as this King right is myne,
For a cross-bow and an arrow,
When I sal come to hunt on Yarrow,
And in token that this thing is sooth
I bit the whyt wax with my tooth,
Before Meg, Maud, and Margery,
And my third sonne Henry. "

At the period of which I write (1798) Montalto was the property of Lord Moira, who commenced to improve his estate in 1770, when he expended upon it some £30,000. This nobleman made many efforts on behalf of his suffering country. In the March and November of 1797 he moved in the British House of Lords that an humble address should be presented to the King, praying him to interpose his parental interference for allaying of the alarming discontents then subsisting in Ireland. " Before God and my country, " said Lord Moira, " I speak of what I myself have seen. I have seen in Ireland the most absurd, as well as the most disgusting, tyranny that any nation ever groaned under. I have seen troops sent full of this prejudice – that every inhabitant of that kingdom is a rebel to the British Government ; the most wanton insults, the most grievous oppressions, practised upon men of all ranks and conditions, in a part of the country as free from disturbance as the city of London. Thirty houses are sometimes burned in a single night ; but, from prudential motives, I wish to draw a veil over more aggravated facts, which I am willing to attest before the Privy Council, or at your lordships' bar. "

These motions were negatived. On the 19th of February, 1798, Lord Moira again brought forward a motion, in the Irish House of Lords, and offered to produce full proof of many acts of barbarous violence ; his motion met the same fate as his previous ones.

On the west side of Ballynahinch and within a few hundred yards of Montalto House, rises the grand old hill of Ednavady, crowded with old Irish earthworks and commanding a magnificent view of the country for miles around and of the quiet little town that nestles at its foot. This was the place chosen by General Monro as the camping ground of the Insurgent army, and no better position could have been chosen. It is said the place was so selected by the Insurgents on account of the patriotic feelings of the Moiras. The hill will ever be an object of interest in consequence of the memorable incidents connected with it, and many a tourist clambers to its summit to look upon the traces of the old entrenchments or feast his eyes upon the beauty of the surrounding scenery. On the centre of the hill-top, enclosed by a high embankment, having a deep trench on either side, is a space capable of accommodating fully a thousand men. From this spot a most extensive view can be obtained, and it commands every approach to Ballynahinch.

The morning of Saturday, the 9th of June, 1798, found the usually quiet little town of Ballynahinch in a state of bustle and commotion. Work was given over ; business suspended ; groups of persons were assembled here and there in eager conversation or consultation. Some hesitated as to which side they should join ; others decided to join neither, and were chiefly concerned in securing their own safety. Goods and furniture were carted and hidden. At many of the doors men stood or sat sharpening their pikes; others, carrying their weapons, were marching towards the camping ground. One incident of an exciting nature occurred during the day. A party of the Castlewellan Yeomanry marched into Ballynahinch, bringing with them a prisoner, arrested under a suspicion of disaffection. The people made a rush at the Yeomanry and secured the prisoner. In the scuffle a Ballynahinch man was killed, and the Yeomanry made off as rapidly as possible.

On the following morning, Sunday, 800 men—horse, foot, and artillery—of the King's troops, marched into Ballynahinch from

Blaris camp. The Argyle Fencibles formed part of the force, and entering the houses helped themselves to whatever they fancied. Breakfast was prepared by one inhabitant, and served out to the soldiers. The colonel, on leaving for Downpatrick, directed a bill to be made out for expense, and said he would see it paid. The bill was afterwards handed to him in Belfast—the *gallant* colonel tore it up and said that that was his answer.

CHAPTER XXXIII.

THE PORTAFERRY ATTACK.

" Rebellion ! foul, dishonouring word,
Whose wrongful blight so oft has stained
The holiest cause that tongue or sword
Of mortal ever lost or gained—
How many a spirit born to bless,
Has sunk beneath that withering name,
Whom but a day's—an hour's success
Had wafted to eternal fame. "—MOORE.

THE total number of United Irishmen enrolled in Ulster has been estimated at 24,000. Barely a third of these rose to follow their leaders and fulfil their pledge.

While the inhabitants of the Northern division of the Ards were assembling, those of a Southern division had marched against Portaferry. Captain Mathews, a man of bravery and experience, had the command of the town. On hearing the unwelcome tidings that a section of the Insurgent army was on its way to attack him he set about making preparations for giving the Patriots a warm reception. The only force at his command was a body of Yeomanry, and the captain placed but little confidence in their courage or skill in warfare ; he was resolved, however, that the Yeomen should fight, whether willing or not.

A revenue cruiser lay in the river at the time ; Mathews directed Captain Hopkins, who had command of her, to bring his guns to bear on Portaferry Street ; then he had the arches of the Market-house filled up with a dry temporary wall, to prevent the Insurgents from setting fire to the loft ; this done, he enclosed his men in the upper portion of the building, and awaited the approach of the enemy.

The object of the Insurgents was to take the town ; then to cross the Ferry, and proceed with whatever reinforcements they might obtain in Lecale, to the attack of Downpatrick. This plan certainly displayed some knowledge of the best tactics to be pursued ; for the presumption was that the garrison of Downpatrick would have marched to join General Nugent at Ballynahinch, and this was actually the case.

When the Insurgents were within a mile of Portaferry they halted at a large and well-stocked public-house, the property of a baronial committee man. They ordered out all that the house contained, and the entire stock rapidly disappeared. The proprietor, observing that the march was about to be resumed, stepped out to one of the leaders and very civilly enquired—

" Wha's tae pay me, sir ? "

There was a shout of laughter at the question, and the only reply the poor fellow obtained was that his country would pay him. A brother of this man was in the ranks, and, on hearing what passed, concluded that he had been long enough in his present company. He accordingly hid himself behind a hedge and allowed his former comrades to proceed without him.

Confident of success, the Insurgents advanced upon Portaferry, flourishing their pikes and cheering loudly. A speedy and bloodless victory they certainly would have achieved but for the foresight of Captain Mathews. As the Ards men approached the Market-house they were met by a volley of musketry. A number of pikemen fell and there was a momentary halt. Again the Ards men advanced, and again they were met with a shower of bullets. At the same moment the shot from the cruiser in the river began to tell ; men dropped in every direction. The pressure in the rere and the exposed situation of the street, together with the uncertainty as to what force was exposed to them, caused a panic and confusion in front, and, unable to return an effectual fire, the Insurgents fled.

Mathews congratulated his men upon their success ; he feared, however, a repetition of the experiment, and no sooner had the Insurgents got clear off than he passed over with his Yeomen to Strangford.

The defeated Insurgents made their way some five or six miles along the shore of Strangford Lough until they came to the residence of Bailey, of Innishargy. One of the Insurgents thus relates what took place there :—

" The airmy lay doon on the lawn, while the offishers tuk possession o' the hoose, whaur they sut doon in the parlour, an' made themsel's free wi' the contents o' the cellar. As they sut enjoyin' themsel's, me and yin or twa mair o' us went up tae the apen wundey and says—' Merry be yer hearts, genteels, an' what'll ye hae the airmy tae drink ? ' ' Hooch,' sez this yin an' that yin, ' there's a water cart in the yerd, tak it doon tae the river an' gie them a drink : ' ' Hech surs, ' sez we, ' is that the wae o' it. Gin we're tae be *soles* an' ye the *uppers* we may jist as weel serve King George.' "

And so from the very outset there were jealousies and divisions amongst the Insurgents as might be expected.

CHAPTER XXXIV.

A PROCLAMATION.

" Lay down your arms, " said Nugent,
" And bring me here Monro,
Or I shall let my bloodhounds out,
And lay each dwelling low ! "—OLD BALLAD.

A REIGN of terror had begun. The town of Belfast was over-crowded by refugees, who from all parts of the country had fled thither for safety. The shops were closed ; the streets and avenues were guarded by the military, and no person was permitted to be upon the streets.

The following proclamation was, on the 11th of June, issued by Major-General Nugent to the inhabitants and Insurgents of County Down : —

" Belfast, 11th June, 1798, 5 p.m.

" Major-General Nugent, commanding his Majesty's forces in the North of Ireland, being desirous of sparing the effusion of human blood, and the total devastation of the County of Down, is pleased to, and does hereby extend, to the Insurgents in said county the same terms of submission and atonement that have been so eagerly and gratefully accepted by many of their equally deluded neighbours in the County of Antrim, to wit :

" That if those unfortunate persons who, by the arts of selfish and designing people, have been seduced from the allegiance to their true and lawful sovereign, his Majesty King George the Third, to become Rebels and Traitors to their country will return to their duty as faithful and peaceable subjects, and to their respective houses and occupations, the General positively and surely engages to them that no one whatever in the county (with the exceptions hereinafter mentioned) shall be molested, or their property injured, and that, as a proof of their return to loyalty and good government, they must, in the course of twenty-four hours after the date of this proclamation (making allowance for more distant parts of the county) liberate all the loyal persons of every description now in their custody, and send them to their respective places of abode, and that they also depute some persons to receive all their arms and offensive weapons of every denomination, with the ammunition belonging thereto, who shall be sent to the General to know where they are to be deposited ; and that they also deliver up the principal persons who have been most active in instigating or compelling them to engage in their late wicked practices.

" Should the above injunctions not be complied with within the time specified, Major-General Nugent will proceed to set fire to and totally destroy the towns of Killinchy, Killyleagh, Ballynahinch, Saintfield, and every cottage and farmhouse in the vicinity of these four places, carry off the stock and cattle, and put everyone to the sword who may be found in arms.

" It particularly behoves all the well-affected persons who are now with the rebels from constraint, and who, it is known, form a considerable part of their numbers, to exert themselves in having these terms complied with, as it is the only opportunity there will be of rescuing themselves and properties from the indiscriminate vengeance of an army necessarily let loose upon them."

A copy of this proclamation found its way into the hands of General Monro, who, with some 7,000 men, was in the neighbourhood of Saintfield. He read it aloud to his army, and the document was greeted with shouts of laughter. Monro immediately despatched one of his officers, named Townshend, to take possession of Ballynahinch. The task was an easy one ; the garrison fled at the approach of Townshend, and the town was taken without bloodshed.

On the 12th Monro, with the remainder of his force, marched for Ballynahinch. On his way he learned that the King's troops, commanded by General Nugent, and supported by General Barber's artillery, had left Belfast to intercept him.

The tidings were true. On that morning Nugent, with 700 infantry, 150 cavalry, and five pieces of cannon, marched from Belfast to attack Monro at Oghley Hill, near Saintfield, where he had been encamped. On arriving there Nugent learned of the departure of the Insurgents for the town of Ballynahinch. He immediately started in pursuit. Before coming upon the Insurgents he was joined by the column under the command of Lieutenant-Colonel Stewart, of the 33rd Regiment, from Downpatrick.

Not far from Montalto Monro awaited the arrival of the military. Their line of approach was painfully visible. As far as the eye could reach the soldiers had fired the country along their line of march.

The two contending forces soon came into collision. For more than an hour Monro was able to keep the Royal forces in check. He had, however, no artillery except a few small ship guns—some six or eight—mounted on country cars, while the British artillery was effective and well served. Monro was at length compelled to give way. He sent instructions to Townshend to evacuate Ballynahinch, a part of which had already caught fire from the falling shells, and drew off his forces to the hill of Ednavady.

In the evening the British troops entered Ballynahinch, and began plundering, burning, and drinking. During the night, exhausted by their orgies, the soldiers lay helpless in the streets. News of the state of affairs was brought to Monro, and a council of war was held. Immediate action was urged by all except Monro. In vain his officers appealed to him to march into the town, and make prisoners of all the drunken soldiers.

" No," said the General, " we scorn to avail ourselves of the ungenerous advantage which night affords ! We will meet them in the blush of day ; we will fight them like men, not under the cloud of night, but the first rays of to-morrow's sun." This fatal mistake of Monro's doing more credit to his heart than his death, was the cause of his overthrow and defeat.

A scene of confusion followed, and a clamour of dissatisfaction was raised. The best-armed division of Monro's men, numbering about 700 were marched off by their leader, and many others deserted also.

During the night nothing worthy of note occurred, but the morning sun ushered in a day of blood and carnage.

CHAPTER XXXV.

THE BATTLE OF BALLYNAHINCH.

" The combat deepens ! On ye brave,
Who rush to glory or the grave ! " —CAMPBELL.

GENERAL NUGENT succeeded in getting possession of the Windmill Hill on the afternoon of the 12th of June. He found the task no easy one to accomplish. His line of march, as he approached Ballynahinch, lay by the side of the steep hill. The ground on each side of the road was divided into small fields, and, from the acclivity of the situation, the fences rose one above the other, forming a kind of amphitheatre. Here Monro had posted some of his best musketeers ambuscaded behind the fences. These were under charge of a young officer named M'Cance, who, throughout entire action, displayed the most steady and determined courage.

No sooner had Nugent, the head of the King's forces, advanced within range of the United army upon the Windmill Hill than he set about dislodging it. Instantly M'Cance opened a fire from his ambuscade and with such effect that the whole British line was interrupted in its advance and kept in check for more than an hour. Nugent lost many men, while the little band of marksmen commanded by M'Cance sustained no injury. Several bold attempts were made by Nugent to storm and carry the Windmill Hill, but so well directed was the fire from its summit that many of the British shewed unwillingness to approach it, and in the case of one particular regiment the utmost exertions of the officers were necessary to induce the men to advance.

Nugent's army now formed between the Windmill Hill and the town of Ballynahinch, presenting front to and directing their fire upon both. Monro was totally defective in cannon ; a few ship guns of small calibre were all he had, and these were of very little service when opposed to the British artillery under General Barber, an efficient and experienced officer.

It was in this posture of affairs that Monro considered it prudent to withdraw his men from the Windmill Hill and to concentrate his entire force on Ednavady, preparatory to a general attack on the British line. He sent orders to M'Cance to retire from the post which he had so ably defended, while Townshend received orders to evacuate Ballynahinch, where some of the houses had caught fire from the discharge of shells.

When the first order to retire reached M'Cance he refused to obey it. A second order came, and he refused, at the same time earnestly pleading for a reinforcement from the Commander-in-chief. A third messenger came bearing the same order. He then quitted his post with reluctance and an agitation of mind which he was unable to conceal.

No sooner did M'Cance quit his post than a British regiment advanced and took possession of it. And here occurred an incident illustrative of the courage and heroism of the Hearts of Down. When M'Cance's men retired from the hill, two of their number were left behind. One had actually refused to quit his post ; the other was suffering from extreme fatigue. He had fought at Saintfield on the 9th, was incessant in every pursuit connected with the duties assigned him, but, exhausted with toil and unable to follow his division, he lay down on the ground and fell asleep. The former, on the advance of the enemy up the hill, maintained his position, and, being a splendid marksman, continued to fire with effect. At last, having discharged his last round, he leaped over the fences and joined his division in safety. The latter was roused from his sleep by the rush of feet over his body. He started up, and was immediately seized upon. He was at once brought before General Nugent, who ordered his instant execution. The brave fellow never flinched. Fixing his bold gaze upon Nugent, he exclaimed—

" I came here to die ; and whether on Ednavady or Windmill Hill can make little difference ! "

" Hang him upon a blade of the old windmill ! " cried Nugent.

The infuriated soldiery were only too glad to have some object upon which to wreak their fury and vengeance. A rope was speedily procured, and in a few minutes the lifeless body of the poor fellow was dangling in the air, suspended to one of the arms of the windmill, where it remained till the close of the following day.

The night was one of deep anxiety with the United army. Harry Monro never thought of seeking rest. He was always on the alert, passing from rank to rank, cheering, encouraging and relieving the wants of his companions.

It was during the night of the 12th that our heroine, Betsy Gray, reached Ednavady. Despite the remonstrances of her father, she carried out her original resolution. Putting a fine mare to an old blockwheel car, and lading the car with cheese, butter, and home-made bread, she started, alone and undaunted, upon her perilous journey. She reached Ednavady in safety, was immediately recognised, and was received with every demonstration of enthusiasm. Her brother and Willie Boal were soon by her side, and the former, in the excitement of the moment, readily forgave his sister for her disobedience of his orders.

The summer of 1798 was a glorious one. It was remarked as a singular circumstance that, during the whole period of the rebellion in Ireland, not a single drop of rain fell. Starry nights and days of brilliant sunshine prevailed. Upon what a scene did the sun look down as he rose from his ocean bed on the morning of the 13th of June ! On the Windmill Hill stood the forces of the King, trained in the ways of warfare ; on the bold summit and sloping sides of Ednavady were thousands of poorly armed and untrained men, prepared to do battle unto the death for the land and the people that they loved. In the valley below slumbered the pretty little town of Ballynahinch.

At the first dawn, Monro formed his men for action, and though their numbers had been sensibly diminished during the night, they betrayed no lack of courage or confidence in their commander.

General Monro commenced the attack by a discharge from eight of his small cannon, which were drawn up against the town. Barber promptly replied by his heavy artillery. A strong division marched from the hill with the view of penetrating the town on the right ; while Monro, in person, headed a more formidable column, directing his march to the left. General Nugent despatched a body of troops to contend the ground with the former, who awaited their approach drawn up in a solid square, and received them with a destructive fire, which checked their advance. The officer commanding the British troops was shot dead ; his men gave way, and retreated hastily back into the town of Ballynahinch.

The men led by Monro displayed great enthusiasm in their advance. They bore down all opposition ; forced an entrance into the town under the most destructive fire of musketry and cannon ; repeated rounds of grape shot sweeping down the whole ranks, which was as rapidly replaced. The pikemen charged to the very muzzle of the guns, and carried off a heavy piece of artillery.

Quite close to Monro, mounted on a magnificent horse, dressed from head to foot in green silk, and waving aloft a slender, glittering sword, to cheer on the men to their deadly work, rode Betsy Gray ! She dashed into the very thickest and hottest of the fight, and, with a heroism that never failed, emboldened the Insurgents by her daring of danger and of death.

Monro's ammunition became exhausted. He gained the very centre of the town, where, exposed to a cross-fire of musketry in the Market Square, and raked by the artillery, he pressed boldly on the enemy with bayonet and pike.

Above the din of musketry and the clash of steel came his cheery cry—

" Charge, lads, for the honour of Down ! "

And they did charge, with a fury so irresistible that Nugent ordered a retreat.

And here followed a scene so extraordinary as to be, perhaps, without a parallel in the history of ancient or modern warfare. Monro's troops, unacquainted with the trumpet's note, and enveloped by the smoke, which prevented them from seeing the hurried movements of the soldiery, mistook the retreat for the signal of charge.

Fatal mistake !

In the very flush of victory, victory bloody but complete, in a hand to hand encounter with trained slayers of men, they turned and fled in one direction just as their enemies were flying in another.

That fatal mistake decided the fate of the day—the fate of the rising in the County Down.

The 22nd Light Dragoons, who had borne no active part in the operations of the day, charged the flying troops of Monro, while the infantry, recovering from their panic, joined in the pursuit.

And now began a series of horrible outrages which shall lie as foul blots upon the history of Ireland through all time.

CHAPTER XXXVI.

A BOY'S REVENGE.

" He suffered bravely, and he fought
The bloody contest through ;
But there remained a something yet
The noble lad could do."—OLD SONG.

THE defeat of the Insurgents was sudden and complete. Nugent's cannon, laden with grape shot, and fired point blank into that mass of human beings which crowded Dromore Street, cut the people down in hundreds, opening up lanes through the crowded ranks, through which, to use the words of an eye-witness, a coach-and-six might have been driven without touching a soul right or left.

In irretrievable confusion, the panic-stricken Insurgents fled in every direction. The town of Ballynahinch was in flames. Only seven of its inhabitants remained in the town. Three of these were burned to death, two were shot down at their own doors, and the other two escaped. The flying Insurgents were mainly composed of men from Bangor, Donaghadee, Newtownards, Greyabbey, Killinchy, and the Cottown. Escape was now their only object, and flinging down their arms they ran for dear life. Some sought refuge in the turf bogs, others lay down amongst the green rushes and waving corn which grew luxuriantly in the surrounding fields, and hundreds were thus saved from the murderous steel of the pursuing horsemen.

The cavalry was mainly composed of the Hillsborough Horse Yeomanry, which was made up of the fiercest and most relentless Protestants from South Down. To it, with the Yeomanry Infantry not engaged till the crisis of the battle, was entrusted the work of pursuit and slaughter. They did their work well, and with brutal ferocity, unequalled by even the bloody dragoons of Claverhouse. Breaking up into small parties of fours or " double threes," and armed with pistols and sabres, they spread themselves over the townlands surrounding Ballynahinch, cutting down, with fiendish savagery, friend and foe alike. Many incidents of the terrible slaughter have been handed down from father to son, and to the present day the bitterest hates exist amongst the descendants of the pursued and pursuers. Two men, named respectively Adair and Mawhinney, natives of Greyabbey, were amongst those who stood in the thickest of the fight. Adair was a wealthy farmer, the owner of considerable property, and a man of note in Greyabbey and neighbourhood, Mawhinney was also a man of means. These two, flinging down their arms, joined in the general flight, and breathless and exhausted had reached Ballykine, when they were pounced upon by a party of the Hillsborough men, who were on a prowl for victims. Unable to proceed further, the poor fellows were easily caught, and the work of murder began. The men were literally hacked to pieces, and Adair was mutilated in a manner too horrible for relation. In an adjoining field, tending his cows, was George Jackson, the owner of the farm upon which this bloody deed had been perpetrated. He was a peaceable and harmless man, loyal to the King, and had resolutely set his face against the rebellion. Thirsting for more blood, the butchers fell upon Jackson, and speedily left him a hacked and disfigured corpse upon his own field. The body of Adair was left in so hideous a condition that those who saw it never forgot the sight. His remains and those of Mawhinney were buried by some friendly hands in a moss field, on Alexander Douglas' land. Adair's grave is about ten yards from the road leading to Lisburn. Some twenty-five years ago the grave was opened—with what object cannot be said. It was found to contain the skeleton of the unfortunate man. Hat, boots and clothing were in a perfect state of preservation. The coat, which was of a superfine green broadcloth, and long skirted, the waistcoat, knee-breeches, and green silk kerchief had suffered but little by their sixty years subjection to the soil under which they and their wearer had been laid. The hat was removed to the Belfast Museum. The clothing was cut into small pieces, and, with the buttons, distributed among the people of the district, who still preserve them as interesting souvenirs of the terrible struggle. Douglas has evinced the utmost reverence for the grave of Adair. With his own hands he built a strong stone structure to the height of about three feet. The grave he covered with verdant sods and planted thereon a sally, which now stands some fourteen feet in height.*

Amongst the flying fugitives was Tommy Burns, the lad who worked in the smiddy of Mat M'Clenaghan, and who was brutally tortured there on the night of the christening. The brave lad, burning to avenge that fearful outrage, accompanied the Granshaw and Cottown men to Ballynahinch, and now he lay by the roadside, alone, weary, hungry, and thirsty. He had fallen asleep, but was aroused by the tramping of feet. Cautiously lifting his head from the dry ditch in which he lay, Tommy saw a company of soldiers marching in his direction. Their bayonets flashed in the sunlight, and, as they drew near, Tommy could hear their shouts of noisy laughter as they discussed the incidents of the recent fight. He was about to crawl into the adjoining field for safety, when his quick eye recognised the features of the officer under whose orders he had been whipped and mutilated at the Six-Road-Ends. Yes, it was he ; jauntily he marched at the head of his men, joining in their laughter, and evidently in the best of humour.

Tommy drew towards him a musket which he had carried in the fight, and examined the priming. It was a clumsy old-fashioned weapon, with which he had brought down many a crow and magpie. He had higher game in prospect now !

* The author of this story has visited the grave of Adair. While there he cut a twig from the sally, and from this twig manufactured the pen-holder which he has used in the writing of this tale.

The soldiers leisurely advanced. When within a dozen paces off Tommy's hiding-place they came, unbidden, to a sudden halt as the lad started from his lair, musket in hand, and faced them upon the roadway.

" What have we here ? " cried the officer, with a laugh.

" Some damned young rebel, you may be sure," replied one of his men.

" Come here, boy ! " said the officer, advancing a pace.

The recognition was now mutual.

" Upon my soul," laughed the officer, " but it's the brat who was cropped by Morris. By God, were he here now, he would have his other ear ! "

The brutal joke was the last the fellow ever uttered. Quick as lightning Tommy raised his musket to his shoulder and discharged it straight in the officer's face. The man's head was literally blown to pieces, and his brains were scattered upon the faces and uniforms of the men nearest to him !

A moment of silent horror followed. Then there was a shout and a rush, and Tommy's body was pierced by a score of bayonets !

CHAPTER XXXVII.

THE SEARCH FOR MONRO.

" Sad is my fate, said the heart-broken stranger ;
  The wild deer and wolf to a covert can flee ;
But I have no refuge from famine and danger,
  A home and a country remain not for me.
Never again in the green sunny bowers,
  Where my forefathers liv'd, shall I spend the sweet hours,
Or cover my harp with the wild-woven flowers,
  And strike to the numbers of Erin go Bragh." — CAMPBELL.

THE town of Lisburn not only supplied the noble and generous-hearted General who commanded the troops of the United Irishmen, but it also played an important part in the short but sanguinary struggle. During the winter of 1797, a shuttle-maker who lived in an entry off High Street, Belfast, worked eighteen hours of the twenty four in making pike heads and handles. He and very many similar experts were, however, outdone by a Lisburn whitesmith who, during the winter of 1797 and the spring of 1798, forged upwards of 500 pikes without leaving undone any of his ordinary work.

Many years before the rebellion of 1798 the Presbyterians of Lisburn had proposed to build a new house of worship. Lord Hertford gave them a handsome site, and subscriptions were collected towards defraying the cost of erection. Amongst the contributors were the Rev. Father Magee, the parish priest and several members of his congregation. Father Magee gave £10, and the donation was very much prized by the Presbyterians. He was exceedingly popular, and, when any works of benevolence were to be performed, he was always beside the Rev. Dr. Cupples, Protestant rector of the parish, and the Rev. Andrew Craig, Presbyterian minister.

There was wonderful excitement in Lisburn and its neighbourhood on the night of the 12th of June, 1798. A report had been circulated that Harry Monro and a large body of his men would that night descend upon the town and destroy it by fire. Soldiers, horse and foot, paraded the streets in large numbers ; the inhabitants were ordered to close their doors and put out their lights after eight o'clock, and every measure was taken to prevent a military surprise. In a house in Market Square sat an Orange Lodge. At a late hour one of the members of this lodge looked out of the door and saw the parish priest making his way homewards. The Orangeman was a member of the Rev. Craig's church, and he had a kindly feeling towards Father Magee, because he remembered his kindness. Stepping up to the clergyman, he said—

" You are out very late, sir, in such troublous times. "

" I am, indeed, my friend, " replied the old gentleman. " I have been out on a sick call. "

" It is a mile to your house, and you can hardly get there in safety, " said the Orangeman ; " our lodge is now sitting, come in for a moment and we'll see about guarding you home. "

The priest entered the lodgeroom, where he was hospitably received, and, having remained there for some time, he was escorted home by four of the members.

On that eventful day numerous arrests were made, and amongst the prisoners were quiet men, who had never joined any political institution. The prisoners were taken to the guard-house, where they were ordered to stand with their backs to the wall of the dark, damp cell, in which position they stood in silent agony and suspense as to what their fate might be.

At the hour of midnight the tramp of a trooper's horse was heard dashing up the street ; the rider pulled up his steed at the prison, held a short conversation with the sergeant of the guard, and then rode off.

No sooner had the trooper ridden off than one of the prisoners put his mouth to the keyhole of the door and cried out—

" For God's sake tell us the news ! "

" My written orders are, " replied the sergeant, " that if a gun be fired in Market Square it will be the signal that the Rebel troops are at hand, and all the prisoners must then be put to death. "

What a night of agony and suspense was that ! Many of the prisoners almost lost their reason. Well for them it was that the rumour concerning Monro was false. Had it been true they would have been butchered in cold blood.

Parties of dragoons and yeomen were sent out into the country in quest of General Monro, and in the course of their search it fared ill with all the persons upon whom they chanced to come. They may have been acting loyally and legally in shooting down persons positively known to be rebels, but these bloodhounds shot at and hewed down nearly every person they met, without asking questions. A party of dragoons, riding from Ballynahinch to Belfast, observed a farmer digging potatoes in his field, near Dundonald.

'" How far is Belfast ? " shouted one of the troopers.

The man was deaf, and, not hearing the question, did not look up.

" He's a rebel, I'm sure, " said the trooper, and raising his carbine he shot the poor man dead.

Near to the same place, the same party seized upon an inoffensive man, and strung him up to a beam which projected from a farm house, where he was strangled to death. That beam was only recently cut down.

A dragoon, immediately after the fight, galloped up to a house, swearing that he would have twenty lives that day before he would sleep for the murder of his brother Billy (a soldier who had been killed near Saintfield). The person thus threatened, with a child on each arm, begged for mercy. The dragoon lifted up his gun, took aim, and pulled the trigger ; but the piece did not go off. When preparing to fire again he observed a man, on his right, running across a field, whom he pursued ; but when leaping a stone fence his horse fell. The rider, however, overtook the man in the next field, and struck him, repeatedly with his sword. The third blow caused him to fall, and when lying, the dragoon cut at him with the point of his sword. When night came two men buried him in a bog, where the grave is still pointed out. The spot, however, is now arable land.

It is well known that the same dragoon killed fifteen men on the day referred to, within half a mile of the house specified. He shot two brothers while they were swimming in Ballykine Lough. He overtook in a field a person named William Fee, and having nearly severed his hand from his wrist, and wounded him severely on the head, another dragoon came up and exclaimed—

" You have given him enough ; come with me. "

A person passing through the field observed the wounded man, who, in the most piteous terms, pleaded for some milk. The person thus addressed, at the risk of his own life, brought him the desired draught. While he was drinking it, his blood was dropping into the vessel. He must afterwards have made his escape during the night, for he was nowhere to be found next morning.

Thirty years afterwards, this man saw a person leaning over a half-door in Weighouse Lane, Belfast, and thought he recognised in him the man to whom he had given the milk. He was confirmed in the opinion he had formed by looking at the wounded wrist. The Ballynahinch man asked him " Do you know me ? " " No, " was the reply. " Well, " continued the other, " I am the man who gave you the bowl of milk on the day that wrist was wounded. " He immediately clasped his benefactor in his arms, brought him into the house and treated him with much kindness.

The blood-thirsty dragoon above alluded to killed a poor simpleton while herding cattle. On the Wednesday morning after the battle, as the rebels were flying in all directions, General Nugent, in giving orders to the dragoons to disperse them, observed, " Now, boys, be merciful. " This was much to the credit of the general ; but, to the disgrace of the soldiers be it told, his orders were by no means strictly obeyed. There was a fearful and indiscriminate slaughter made during the afternoon of the battle. While passing the house of a farmer in Ballylone, the dragoons stopped and asked for milk. Basins of cream were carried out to them. One of the soldiers remarked " He (the master of the house) is a rebel ; look at the cloth round his hand ; he has been wounded in the battle. " On uttering these words, the trooper shot the ill-fated farmer. He and his family were staunch Loyalists. Before leaving the dying man, the rest of the soldiers examined his hand, and found, instead of the suspected wound, only a common boil, over which a bandage had been rolled. On seeing this, one of the party said to his comrade who had fired the fatal shot, " I'll never remain in the company with such a murderer. " For his bloody deed, the inhuman soldier was tried by a court-martial, and is reported to have been shot in Belfast.

The dragoons, when " scouring the country, " entered houses and hacked the cheese with their bloody swords.

They frequently seized the farmers' horses, pretending to take them away, and exacting five or ten pounds for their return. Two young men from Newtownards left the rebels on the evening of Wednesday, and saw no way of escaping but by giving themselves up to the Yeomanry stationed on the hill in the rere of the Third Presbyterian Church. The Yeomen had just taken them under their protection, when some dragoons galloped up the hill, and seeing the young men, shot one of them in the presence of the captain. A soldier standing by resolved to kill the other, but, having no weapon, lifted up a long piece of nailrod, bent it in the middle, and was in the act of rushing forward to put the two ends into the rebel's eyes when the captain interposed. The young man thus saved was protected by the Yeomen for three days, and afterwards reached home in safety. A few days before the fight, a person in Ballynahinch had a party of rebels in his house drinking. Observing some Yeomen passing, the Insurgents resolved on making them prisoners. One of them caught hold of a gun in the hands of a Yeoman, and, while wrestling for it, was shot. The Yeomen were then captured, and a guard placed over them. The sentinel afterwards fled to Newry ; but, being recognised by one of the men over whom he had kept watch, he was apprehended, tried, and condemmed to death. He being a tall and handsome youth, the colonel offered him his freedom, provided he would renounce his rebellious principles and join the army. He firmly refused, observing " You have hung my father ; you may do the same to me. " At the place of execution, he ran up the ladder, and fixing his head in the noose of the rope, he flung himself off without the aid of the hangman.

A United Irishman, who gave his name as Crabbe, was the first person hanged for treason in Lisburn. He suffered death on a lamp-post at the corner of Castle Street, and right opposite the Market-house. The charge against him was that of having a pistol in his pocket and a green cockade hidden in his hat. Some reports went to say that he had been a clergyman, but no direct proof of the fact was ever brought forward, nor did a single secret connected with his history transpire, from that day to the present. He was taken prisoner in one of the bye-lanes in Lisburn, and in three hours afterwards was tried, convicted, and executed. A very fine looking man, named Armstrong, was at the same time taken into custody. Several letters were found sewn up in the inner lining of his waistcoat, and the contents of these communications shewed that he must have been engaged in the proceedings of the Insurgents. As in all other cases, the members of the military court were very easily satisfied respecting a prisoner's guilt, and promptitude in trying persons being very popular, their deliberations were short, and conclusions were rapidly arrived at. Norbury himself, bloodthirsty as he was, never delighted more in the destruction of human life than the members of the court-martial at Lisburn.

Armstrong was sentenced to die, but in the hope of exacting private information from the condemned man, he was told by persons in authority that if he gave full information of all he knew respecting the Insurgent leaders his life would be spared, and a large reward bestowed upon him. To strengthen this proposal, or rather to give greater force to the temptation, his wife was sent to him, and the poor woman, in the frenzy of her affection, flung herself on her knees before her husband, beseeching him to accept the terms. Terrible was the struggle of the poor fellow under this trying appeal ; but after a moment's thought, his firmness, which had partly forsaken him, returned with renewed strength, and no influence could be brought to induce him to give any information likely to inculpate his comrades. " My life," he said, " is only one, and God will watch over my widow and children. Were I to become informer, torrents of blood would be shed, numbers of wives would be made widows, and hundreds of children left fatherless. In after days many persons may brand me as a rebel, but no one will dare to say that I was a traitor." No matter what opinion may be held as to the righteousness of the cause for which Armstrong suffered ; every honourable minded man will, however, admit that in this instance he displayed dignity sufficient to throw a halo round his memory, and that under all the circumstances his death was that of a hero. Armstrong came from Tullyrush, where he now lies buried.

Whole volumes might be filled with romantic incidents both as regards deeds of mercy and doings of darkness.

The little town of Hillsborough was the theatre of many tragic scenes. This ancient stronghold had for at least two centuries been famed as a military depot, and to the present the head of the house of Hill retains the title of Chief Constable of the Fort. The uniform worn by castle men who are supposed to do duty there is that of the antiquated style worn by the Dutch guards which formed the personal staff of William the Third. Hillsborough lies convenient to Blaris, where for several years before and after the breaking out of the rebellion, a camp of soldiers was quartered, and detachments of those troops guarded the town all that period. Immediately after the fight at Ballynahinch, a party of dragoons—that had been ordered to search the country and seize all stragglers likely to have been engaged in the battle—overtook a lad eighteen years of age, and who travelled on his way towards Hillsborough. He turned out to be a weakminded creature, most unlikely to have carried arms or taken part in the recent warfare, but on being interrogated by the troopers he stated without hesitation that he had witnessed the battle, and that he fled from the scene of strife with the United army. This confession was considered quite sufficient to justify his arrest, and he was dragged into Hillsborough tied to the saddle of one of the dragoons. After his arrival in the town he was tried, and found guilty, for having taken part with the rebels, although it appeared quite evident that his visit to Ballynahinch had been one of mere curiosity. But the fiat was pronounced, he was led to the church gate—the Tyburn of the town—where speedy preparations were made for his execution.

While this part of the tragedy was being enacted the poor simpleton looked on with the utmost unconcern, never for a moment supposing that the dragoons really intended to take his life ; and even when the cord was placed around his neck he said—" Now boys, ye're jist makin' too much iv the joke." But scarcely had he uttered the words when two stout soldiers caught the end of the cord which had previously been thrown over the top rail of the gate and commenced to pull with all their might. In a moment the imbecile was hauled up several feet from the ground writhing in the death gasp, amid the jeers and mocks of the savage spectators.

Next day a poor looking traveller, weary and footsore, was passing down the hill leading through the same town, and in the direction of Belfast. The sergeant of the guard went up to him and put the usual questions, in reply to which the stranger said he had come from Dublin, on his way to Derry. Not being satisfied with this statement, the sergeant brought him to the lock-up, a small room used as a temporary guard-house by the Dromore Yeomanry then stationed in Hillsborough. Some slight refreshment was given to the prisoner, after which he begged permission to throw himself on a bed in one corner of the room. The request was granted, and in a few minutes the fatigued prisoner fell sound asleep. While he slumbered one of his shoes dropped off, and was picked up by a soldier of the local infantry, who, on examining it, found concealed between the inner and outer sole a medal, or " pass," which proved the owner to have been concerned with the United Irishmen. On finding this symbol, the Yeoman handed it to his superior officer. An impromptu court had been sitting at the time, and the mysterious medal, having been duly examined, was considered sufficient proof of guilt. The man was immediately aroused from that rude couch to learn that he had been tried and condemned, and in fifteen minutes afterwards his lifeless body swung from the very spot at which, twenty-four hours before, the poor idiot had suffered a felon's death. An antiquarian has in his possession the rebel pass which was found in the shoe of that unfortunate traveller. It is made of copper ; in size it is about that of a penny piece of the old coinage. The obverse has the words, " May Orr's fate nerve the impartial arm to avenge the wrongs of Erin." On the reverse there appears the Irish harp with the spear and cap of freedom, and the motto " Liberty—remember William Orr."

CHAPTER XXXVIII.

THE BETRAYAL OF MONRO.

" With sinking mind and bosom riven,
And heart with lonely anguish aching,
It needs my long-taught hope in heaven
To keep that weary heart from breaking ! "—GRIFFIN.

IMMEDIATELY after the battle of Ballynahinch the followers of Monro were scattered like sheep, and fled in all directions. The unfortunate general, though sadly broken down by fatigue, and dispirited by defeat, was the last to leave the field ; nor did he finally abandon the scene until, as he had hoped, the remnant of his people had got into some place of comparative safety. For several hours Monro roamed about the country, and though well-known by many of the farmers, the large rewards offered for his apprehension failed to induce any of them to betray him. One of the Loyalists concealed him for nearly two days, and bestowed on him all possible kindness. But as the harbouring of any suspected person was at that time an offence of great magnitude, the hospitable entertainer of Monro dare not run the risk of allowing him to stop at his place for any lengthened time, especially as patrols of cavalry were marching through the country on the look-out for straggling men of the routed army. On the morning of the 15th June, Monro was obliged to leave his shelter, and, at the break of day, he started in search of another hiding-place.

The adverse fate which pursued Monro led him to a farmstead occupied by a man named Billy Holmes, and situated in Clintina-goold, on the borders of Dromara, and two and a half miles from Bally-nahinch. Five pounds in cash and a small parcel of clothes was all the property then in the possession of General Monro, and this he handed to Holmes as a reward for his concealment until the opinion of Government should be known. The fellow willingly accepted the gift, and expressed the utmost sympathy for the fugitive. Having made sure of the cash and the clothes, Holmes gave Monro some re-freshment, and then led him to what he assured him would be a safe place of concealment. This was a crew and in it Holmes covered Monro with bundles of straw, assured him of his safety, and left him to his exhausted slumbers.

Holmes and his wife were cruel hosts, damnably did they betray their wearied guest. They did not for a single moment purpose keeping faith with Monro, and no sooner was the General in his place of hiding than they set about thinking how to make the most of his secret. With this view Holmes' wife started off for Hillsborough, the nearest seat of military authority. Here she met four members of the local corps of Yeomanry, known as the Black Troop, as they wore no uniform save a band of white linen round the left arm. To these men she reported what had occurred. They immediately armed themselves with muskets and bayonets, and, guided by Holmes' wife, proceeded to the hiding-place of Monro. As soon as they arrived there they captured their prey and tied his hands behind his back. Monro, finding himself betrayed, bitterly reproached his betrayers, and then sought to soften his captors by stating that if they allowed him to go free his friends would pay them a large sum.

The Yeomen, however, were not to be tempted. Hoping for a higher reward than Monro could give, they refused to make terms with him, and in great triumph they marched their prisoner into Dromore, where he was lodged in the house of Brush, the agent, now the Rectory.

What reward the fellows received is not known, but their miserable fate is no secret. Every one of the four possessed, at the time of the arrest, some property, yet they afterwards became miserably poor, and the longest lived of the four died a pauper.

A worse fate was reserved for Holmes. Stung by an accusing conscience, he dragged out a miserable existence. From the day on which he violated his faith to the last hour of his life he was despised for his deceit, and denounced for his treachery, and he was held in scorn and contempt by people of every class and creed in his neighbourhood, shunned in private life, and avoided in the Market Place. When he felt the hour of death approaching he sent for the Presbyterian clergyman who ministered to the congregation of which he was an unworthy member. He did so, it is believed, in order that he might make full confession of his base deed. When the clergyman arrived, Holmes requested his family and friends to leave the room, as he had something important to tell his minister. They refused to do so, and the creature died, a wretched outcast, and with the stain of the foul deed upon his soul. His descendants to the present day, although not bearing his name, have the slur cast in their teeth. His grave and that of his wife's are unmarked, yet dishonoured in Dromara churchyard.

CHAPTER XXXIX.

THE EXECUTION OF MONRO.

" Far dearer the grave or the prison,
  Illum'd by one patriot name,
Than the trophies of all who have risen
  On Liberty's ruins to fame ! " -MOORE.

THE military authorities of Hillsborough ordered out a strong guard, and under this, Monro, handcuffed, was marched from Dromore to Lisburn, where he was confined for the night in a temporary prison in Castle Street.

When his friends learned of his arrest, the utmost sympathy was shewn for him. His clothes were torn, and his health had suffered much from the fatigue he had undergone. George Whitla, a Lisburn cotton manufacturer, sent him a full suit of clothes, while his clerygman, the rector of the parish, Rev. Dr. Cupples, who resided within a few doors of the guard-house, had his meals carried to him from the rectory during the period of his confinement.

On Monday, the 17th June, the trial came on before a court-martial, composed of officers belonging to the several regiments then lying in Lisburn Barracks and at Blaris Camp. Amongst those officers, General Goldie, who was an Orangeman, and his aide-de-camp, M'Coy, were characterised as men of great austerity. In one case it is said that when a rebel soldier was about to suffer M'Coy pushed him up the ladder. The tribunal before which Monro was tried sat in a large room situate near the guard-house ; and it is only fair to state that, if mercy rarely found a resting place in that august assembly, justice was rigidly enforced. Short was the period of the court's deliberations ; it required little proof to convict, and it was still easier to condemn. Only three witnesses were examined for the Crown, and the deposition that the prisoner had led the native troops at the recent battles being conclusive, the sentence of death was at once written out, and Harry Monro was ordered for execution.

Monro was immediately informed that he had not long to live, and to make speedy preparation for the death that awaited him. On his way from the judgment-hall to the place of punishment he requested to be taken to the rectory, that he might receive the sacrament. That rite of the Church having been administered to him, he was led down the street to the Market Square, where a temporary gallows had been erected in front of Ward's stationery warehouse, and nearly opposite his own dwelling house. He was dressed in a black coat, nankeen knee-breeches, and white stockings. A guard of the 23rd Light Dragoons, under Colonel Wollarston, and two companies of the local Yeomanry, were drawn up before the place of execution. During all the preliminary arrangements the condemned patriot exhibited perfect calmness and resignation. One request alone he made and this was while the executioner adjusted the fatal noose—to beg the commanding officer's permission to see a friend who resided in the immediate vicinity of the spot where he stood. That request was granted, and when the man appeared he addressed a few words to him in a low tone just before he ascended the ladder leading to the gallows. What he said on the occasion was never known by the relations of the friend into whose ear it was spoken. The moment preparations had been made, Monro stepped from the street up the ladder, but the slight rung on which he alighted having given way, he fell down against some of the guards by whom he was surrounded. Recovering his balance in a moment, although having his arms firmly pinioned, he said, "All right, " and refusing assistance, again mounted the ladder. When he had reached the required height, the executioner, whose face was closely veiled by a piece of black crape, also ascended to the spot, and placed the rope round the prisoner's neck with an awkwardness of manner that proved him to be a mere amateur in the art of legal strangulation. Without waiting for the final act of the finisher of the law, the doomed one suddenly leaped forward, and as the body fell and swung to and fro, a low wail of sorrow, which the military authorities vainly endeavoured to repress, told how bitterly the tragic end of their fellow-townsman was felt by the multitude that thronged the place of execution. Many of his acquaintances—many linen merchants, who in happier days had stood side by side with Harry Monro in the Linen Hall, engaged in the usual pursuits of their business—were around him in his last moments. And, though several of these looked upon his conduct as that of misguided patriotism, his political opponents, as well as his personal friends, mourned heartily over the sad fate of the man whom every one respected as a worthy and amiable citizen. When the body was taken down, the final vengeance of the law had not been fully satisfied—the authorities, who irresponsibly wielded the powers of life and death, having ordered that decapitation should take place after the execution of the first part of the sentence. On that savage act having been perpetrated, a dragoon seized the head and flung it into the air, shouting, " There goes the head of a traitor. " In this act of wanton ferocity the operator seemed to think that, in thus outraging the remains of an unfortunate fellow-creature, he performed an achievement worthy the glory of a British soldier. Monro's head, with the white night-cap still on it, was afterwards stuck on a pike, and placed on the front of the Market-house—the military authorities carrying out a custom barbarous as any ever practised by the most savage tribes of the New Zealanders. Some weeks afterwards a Scotch nobleman, passing through the town, and feeling shocked at the disgraceful spectacle, had the head taken down and interred in the Lisburn churchyard, in the same grave that contained the other portion of the mutilated body.

After the death of Harry Monro many of the disaffected party were made prisoners, and lodged in the Lisburn Guard-house. Two of these people were tried and convicted, the sentence of death following close on the verdict of guilty. One of the condemned was Richard Vincent, copper and tin smith, a native of Lisburn, and the other was named Maxwell. These men were executed almost immediately after receiving sentence, and their heads, after being cut off, were placed on the Market-house beside Monro's. Not many days after his execution, a sister of the general (one who had been celebrated as a heroine in the national struggle) was passing through the town, and when opposite the Market-house she gazed for a moment at her brother's head, and exclaimed aloud, " Ah, Harry, you will be avenged for all yet ! "

A soldier's hands held the axe by which Monro's head was struck off. With the blood still reeking on its blade, the soldier rushed into a marine store kept in Lisburn by a Mrs. Griffin, and, throwing down the weapon, demanded for it the price of a naggin of whiskey. The woman regarded the bloody instrument with feelings of horror, but knowing how dangerous it was in those days to refuse compliance to the demands of a soldier, she gave threepence to the man, who left with her the hatchet and departed.

On the same day a Glassdrummond farmer, named Thomas Murray, was in Lisburn selling peats. He called on Mrs. Griffin, and the poor woman begged him to take away the hatchet, as neither luck nor grace could follow the house that gave it shelter. Murray gave her a bag of turf in exchange for the axe, and sold the latter for seven and sixpence to Hugh Duncan, a carpenter in Glassdrummond. His son, James Duncan, had the axe long in his possession, showing it to the writer of this story. It is now in the possession of the Richardsons of Lissue.

CHAPTER XL.

THE FATE OF BETSY GRAY.

" Shame on the cruel, ruthless band
Who hunted down to death their prey !
And palsy strike the murderous hand
That slew the lovely Betsy Gray !"—OLD BALLAD.

IT is time to return to our heroine.

When the last hope of the Insurgents had vanished, Betsy Gray, her brother, and lover fled along the Lisburn Road. It was decided that she should dismount from her horse and flee on foot, as there would thus be a better chance of eluding observation. The three had reached a place called Ballycreen, Betsy leading by a couple of hundred yards. She had gained a piece of high, rocky land, where she would be safe from the approach of cavalry, and here she awaited the arrival of Willie Boal and her brother George.

But the murderers were upon the track !

A party of Hillsborough heroes had been in hot pursuit of the three, and gained rapidly upon them. Before George Gray and young Boal could reach Betsy's hiding-place they heard the Yeomen in their rear shouting to them to surrender. The poor fellows were weary with running, and their strength was well nigh spent. The shouts came nearer. Suddenly Boal stopped.

" George, " he said, " let us surrender. By so doing we may save Betsy's life and our own too. If we continue to fly we may betray her hiding-place, and she may be destroyed. "

" Come on, " urged George, seizing Boal by the arm ; " they would never lay violent hands upon a woman. "

" Ay, that they would ! " exclaimed Boal, " and here I stay. "

As he spoke he turned round and faced the pursuers.

" Be it so, " said George ; " we will stand or fall together. "

In a few moments the Yeomen, flushed and breathless, were face to face with the two unarmed men. Without a single word they fell upon them with their swords. George, for a moment or two evaded the thrusts of the Yeomen's weapons, but Boal, less fortunate, received a stab in his neck. He uttered a wild cry, and dashing forward seized his foe by the throat.

That cry reached the ear of Betsy Gray, and she recognised the voice. Springing from her concealment she bounded over an intervening hedge, and the next instant was with her friends. She found her lover dying upon the ground, and her brother struggling with a fellow by whom he had been wounded. One of the Yeomen was just about to plunge his sword into George's body from behind. Betsy grasped the weapon in her naked hands, and madly strove to wrench it from the fellow's grasp.

" Mercy ! " she cried ; " if you are men, spare my brother's life. "

Her appeal was in vain !

At the sound of her voice George turned round and begged of her to fly.

" Never ! " exclaimed Betsy. " Oh, for my trusty blade now, that I might avenge the murder of my poor Willie ! "

Even as she spoke she was set upon by three of the ruffianly band. One of them struck her upon the wrist with his sword, cutting her hand completely off ; another put his pistol close to her eyes and sent a bullet crashing through her brain. At the same instant her brother was shot, and the three brave, but unfortunate, companions lay bleeding upon the green sod.

Even then the butchers were not satisfied. While some of them hacked and hewed the quivering bodies of George Gray and Willie Boal, others of them desecrated the corpse of Betsy. They stripped her of nearly all her clothing, and one brute tore her ear-rings from her ears and the rings from off her fingers.

A more brutal deed has never been recorded. An officer, who came up shortly after the dastardly Yeomen had decamped in search of fresh victims, gazed long and earnestly at the dead body of Betsy Gray.

" A fairer face I have never looked upon, " exclaimed the soldier, " and, by Heavens, the fellow who slew her is a murderer of the blackest dye ! "

The names of some of the participators in the foul deed are well known, they were from Anahilt. To the day of their death they were abhorred and avoided as a pestilence, alike by Orange and Green, Protestant and Catholic, saint and sinner. Their descendants suffer for the deeds of their ancestors, as till the present day they share the odium which justly attached to the cowardly and bloodthirsty scoundrels, who slew a lovely and defenceless woman and two helpless and unarmed men.

The story has been recorded by the historian, and sung by the poet; a ballad, of which the following is a copy, is still familiar in thousands of homes :—

BETSY GRAY.

A BALLAD OF NINETY-EIGHT.

OH, many a noble lad and lass
Who joined the fight of ninety-eight,
To right the cruel wrongs of years,
Did meet with sad and bloody fate.

On Ednavady's sloping heights,
In June, upon the thirteenth day ;
In thousands stood the Patriots bold,
To fight for home and victory.

But bravest of them all, I ween,
Who mustered there upon that day,
And drew the sword for fatherland
Was lovely, winsome Betsy Gray.

From Granshaw, near to Bangor town,
With Willie Boal that day she came ;
Her brother, too, was by her side,
Inspired by patriotic flame.

And when the tide of battle raged,
And showers of bullets fell around,
Still in the thickest of the fight
Was noble-hearted Betsy found.

When adverse fate with victory crowned
The loyal host upon that day,
Poor George and Willie joined the flight,
And with them lovely Betsy Gray.

Along the Lisburn Road they fled,
Pursuing Yeomen keeping watch ;
Then Betsy drew her gleaming sword
And hid it in a farmhouse thatch.

She reached the vale of Ballycreen—
Her friends some distance were behind—
And quickly did she look around
A quiet hiding-place to find.

But, ere 'twas found, she heard a cry,
Alas ! too well she knew the sound ;
Her brother and her sweetheart true
Had by the Yeoman band been found !

Then from the grassy vale she sprang—
This beauteous, noble, fearless maid—
And back she ran with bounding step,
That she might seek to give her aid.

Ah, what a sight then met her gaze !
Her Willie weltering in his gore,
And George, her brother, by his side,
Pleading for life in accents sore.

A Yeoman raised his sword to strike,
As Betsy to the rescue ran—
" Oh, spare my brother's life ! " she cried,
" Oh, spare him, if you be a man ! "

She raised her white and rounded arm
As if to ward the dreaded stroke ;
Vain was her prayer—the weapon fell
And smote her hand off as she spoke.

Another of the murderous crew,
A man who came from Anahilt,
Laughed at the brutal deed and cried—
" More rebel blood must yet be spilt ! "

He drew a pistol from his belt,
And shot poor Betsy in her eye ;
She sank upon the heathery mound,
And died without a sob or sigh.

That night the murdered three were found
By Matthew Armstrong—then a lad,
Who, quickly running to his home,
Related there his tidings sad.

No tombstone marks that humble grave,
No tree nor shrub is planted there ;
And never spade disturbs the spot
Where sleeps the brave, where rests the fair.

Shame on the cruel, ruthless band
Who hunted down to death their prey ;
And palsy strike the murderous hand
That slew the lovely Betsy Gray !

CHAPTER XLI.

BETSY'S GRAVE.

" No tombstone marks that humble grave,
No tree nor shrub is planted there ;
And never spade disturbs the spot
Where sleeps the brave, where rests the fair. "

IN the farm of Samuel Armstrong, of Ballycreen, within two miles of Ballynahinch, lies a picturesque and beautiful little dell, surrounded by rocks and furze, and hidden from the eye of the traveller upon the adjacent roads.

Not far from this secluded spot was enacted the tragedy described in the foregoing chapter. On the morning of the murder, a lad named Matthew Armstrong (uncle of Samuel Armstrong) came upon the dead and mutilated bodies of Betsy Gray, her brother, and lover. He informed two farmers, named respectively Anthony Orr and Wm. Graham, of his discovery, and accompanied them to the spot. The sight was a harrowing one. The three bodies lay quite close together, gory and disfigured. Tenderly lifting Betsy in their arms, they bore her to the little vale upon Armstrong's farm, and, having procured spades, dug for her a grave in the turf-covered soil. Here she was laid, lovingly and gently ; her blood-stained locks smoothed down, and her disordered clothing—or such of it as had not been torn away by her ruthless slayers—adjusted. In the same grave were laid her brother and her lover, and then, with tear-dimmed eyes, the kindly farmers shovelled in the earth, piled up the green sods, and departed homeward, leaving those faithful Hearts of Down sleeping the sleep that knows no waking, till that last morn when earth and sea shall yield up their dead.

Over a century has passed since the bright June sun looked down upon the fresh sods that covered these noble hearts. Expectant friends would await their return in vain ; the old home in Granshaw would see them no more for ever. Neither spade nor plough has ever disturbed that hallowed spot. The people of the district regard it with the deepest reverence, and often as they visit the place, they sit upon the emerald sod and recall the story which has been handed down from father to son. A log of black oak thrown across the head of the grave alone marks the spot, and this is so grown over by the grass as to be scarcely noticeable.

The sword which Betsy carried is still in existence. In the course of her flight the poor girl plunged the weapon up to the hilt in the thatch of a farm cottage, doubtless expecting that some day she would return to claim it. The weapon was soon afterwards discovered by the farmer who occupied the cottage, and he carefully hid it away as a precious relic of the struggle of '98. In the year 1839 two packmen, named John Andrews and Alick Alexander, in the course of their peregrinations, called at this same cottage, and spread before the farmer's wife their tempting wares. The woman fancied a shawl, but she had not the money to pay for it. The men, anxious to do business, suggested barter, but for a time the woman could not think of anything which she could offer in exchange. At length she thought of the sword of Betsy Gray. Producing the weapon from its hiding-place, she related the story connected with it, and offered it in payment of the coveted shawl. The bargain was at once closed. It was not without some misgivings that the woman parted with the sword, for she dreaded the anger of her husband, and insisted upon one of the packmen concealing the much-prized trophy in his umbrella lest it should be seen by the farmer, who was at work in an adjoining field.

The men left, satisfied with their day's work ; and, making their way into Ballynahinch, they secured lodgings and ordered supper. While the meal was being cooked they examined the sword, and chuckled as they thought of the price they could obtain for it from their employer, one Lindsay, of Kilmarnock, in Scotland ; a man who was the possessor of quite a museum. Their dialogue was interrupted by the hasty entrance of a man, who turned out to be the owner of the sword, and who, having discovered his wife's act, had started out in pursuit of the packmen. He fiercely flung down the shawl at their feet and demanded the return of his valued trophy. The men refused, and an angry altercation followed. A few glasses of whiskey, a hearty supper, and pair of new boots bestowed upon the farmer, softened his heart, and he confirmed the sale of the sword, which soon afterwards found its way into the hands of Lindsay. That gentleman's son, Sergeant David Lindsay, of Mount Royal, Portrush, is at present the possessor of this interesting relic of '98, and it is shown by him to many who are curious to see and touch the blade which was so bravely wielded on that memorable 13th of June, 1798, by the beautiful and brave hearted heroine of the Battle of Ballynahinch, whose ashes repose 'neath the verdant turf of the vale of Ballycreen.

CHAPTER XLII.

THE EXECUTION OF WARWICK.

" Out of the tyrant's power ! Free from the scourge of the rod !
Gone to a holier region ; safe with the martyr's God. " —LYTTLE.

THE name of Warwick will be remembered in Down as long as that of Orr will be recollected in Antrim. For fully six months he had been a prisoner at large. Bitterly did he lament the cruel fate which had befallen his faithful friend Betsy and her companions. Of himself he thought not, little dreaming of the storm which was soon to burst on his unfortunate head. He fully expected, as did all his friends, that he would be pardoned, so trifling was the offence which had been laid to his charge. It was to be otherwise, and his persecutors were to have the satisfaction of spilling his innocent blood upon the scaffold.

Brief was the notice given him that the awful sentence was to be carried out ; short was the time allowed him to prepare for the terrible ordeal, and to bid farewell to his many friends, to tear himself away from his grey-haired mother and his darling sweetheart.

Monday, the 15th of October, 1798, was the day fixed for Warwick's execution. The morning was dark and lowering, the sun hid his face, and nature seemed shrouded in mourning for the scene about to be enacted.

A troop of horse and a battalion of infantry were mustered in front of the provost in which Warwick was imprisoned. Many friends were seen clustered in small parties about the Square in Newtownards, and a carriage in which the devoted victim of the times was to be conveyed to the place of execution stood opposite the windows of the room. His friends were admitted singly to pay their final visit and say a last farewell. Warwick was greatly agitated ; his accustomed serenity and self-command had forsaken him entirely. In the centre of the room stood a table on which were scattered a few books. Beside them was a neatly tied up and labelled parcel ; it contained a number of confidential and domestic papers ; the signature of the president of the court-martial was written outside. The packet also contained several letters, which were seized on the arrest of Warwick, and which were from his loved Mary. Poor Mary ! She lay in a violent convulsive fit in the arms of her aged father, who had borne her to a dark corner of the prisoner's apartment. They had spent the greater part of the night together in reading and in consoling each other under the dreadful visitation that was about to alight on both. Warwick had just been pressing her to his bursting heart ; he had received from her an assurance of her everlasting fidelity, which was ratified by an embrace of love and honour ; in an agony of despair she had swooned away, and taking advantage of the temporary absence of the powers of perception, he laid her gently in her father's arms and with a manly resolve prepared to quit the room and to meet death with the indignation of an injured patriot, yet with the firmness and resignation of a true Christian.

Warwick paused for a moment as he was about to depart, and cast his eyes again towards the angel of his earthly existence, as she lay insensible to all that was to happen, her pale and beautiful face marked with the lines of deep sorrow. As he did so he calmly said—

" I do not complain ; God's will must be done ; but the vengeance of man is surely more terrible than even the visitations of the Almighty. Our Heavenly Father is of long suffering and slow to anger ; but man is sudden and furious in his revenge. To die is appalling, even under any circumstances, but to be separated from her with whom I had hoped to enjoy many years of love and happiness ; to be dragged down to the grave thus early in life, and to leave her behind who is to me all that belongs to life itself. O, God ! support me in this terrible hour of my dark despair."

In a fit of wildness and fearful agitation he clasped his aching forehead, his frenzied eyes speaking volumes of inward torture, and rushing out, flung himself into the carriage which was prepared for him, whilst the closing in of the soldiery, the prancing of the troopers, the slow and solemn tread of the guards, and the marching orders of the officers drowned from the ears and shut out from the eyes of Warwick's friends what his tortures must have been, and the cavalcade departed for the place of execution.

The echo of the departed procession was no longer heard in the lonely street when the unfortunate Mary gave signs of returning animation. Her father bore her to the open window, that the cooling breezes of the morning might assist returning nature. But with return of life there was no return of reason. The eyes were glazed, her features rigid, and she looked on those around her as though nothing but empty space was there. Then it was that the soul of the father was in terrible tribulation. He did not weep, but he groaned heavily in mental agony.

When the procession reached Mountstewart a scene was enacted sufficient " to make even angels weep." The Marquis of Londonderry, who had presided at Warwick's trial, had been the one who a short time before hanged the Rev. James Porter, the Presbyterian Minister of Greyabbey, in front of his own manse, was just about to mount his horse to see that the sentence of the court was fulfilled to the letter, when his invalid daughter, a wasted and lovely girl, wrapped up in a portion of her bed-clothes, rushed from the splendid hall, and flinging herself on her knees on the green sward, begged the life of the devoted victim. The judge was inexorable ! The law must be obeyed, and the next funeral wail, after poor Warwick's, that rose on the shores of Loch Cuan, was heard over the departed daughter of the cruel father of Lord Castlereagh, who ended his life with his own hand.

The apparatus of death was erected close by Kirkcubbin meeting-house. Three files of soldiery, flanked by the troopers, surrounded Warwick and his friends. Some members of the Presbytery were with him, and in particular the hoary and venerable minister of Kirkcubbin stood by his young friend addressing himself in frequent prayer to the throne of righteousness and mercy.

The morning all along had been exceedingly stormy and wet. A gigantic mass of heavy thunder-clouds gathered immediately over the heads of the party. The Rev. Brydon had just finished his touching appeal to God, when a frightful peal of thunder burst right above the crowd, and all around seemed one great sheet of fire. The stern troopers looked on each other with amazement, and all save the chief and the devoted Warwick trembled like the quivering leaves of the surrounding wood. How different were the feelings which produced that self-command in these two men ! In Warwick the power of religion and a heart of purity and innocence, bore him up even in the bitter hour of death. In Londonderry all his brutal nature was summoned up to stifle conscience. The storm continued unabated. The rain fell down in torrents ; the lightning blazed more frightfully ; the thunder shook the firmament as if a revolution were at hand ; and in the midst of these convulsions of nature Warwick was sacrificed to appease unnatural vengeance. Just as he was in his last convulsive struggle, a small cloud that had detached itself from the heavy masses above descended as though it would alight on the head of the dying man. It opened, and, to the amazement of everyone present, a white dove was seen, with downward wing hovering immediately over the gallows tree. In another moment the cloud closed on the airy messenger and all was over with poor Warwick. Londonderry waved his sword, the ranks opened, and spurring his horse he rode off at a gallop to Mountstewart, looking dismayed and disheartened.

Wonder sat on every brow. The body was cut down, and as it was lowered to the earth the Rev. Brydon fearlessly exclaimed :—

" Out of the power of tyranny ! "

The remains of Warwick rest in Movilla graveyard, Newtownards. His broken-hearted mother decked his grave with flowers, and every day during the remainder of her life she visited the mournful spot. An eye-witness has thus described the scene often witnessed by him unobserved and at a respectful distance : " The frail old woman, with wrinkled features and white hair, kneeling upon the grave, her hands clasped, her weeping eyes turned up to Heaven, and her quivering lips moving in silent prayer."

And these things happened in the County Down a little over one hundred years ago !

CHAPTER XLIII.

CONCLUSION.

I HAVE but little more to tell my readers regarding the struggle of '98 in County Down. Volumes could be filled in recounting deeds of blood ; the publication of these, however, might but perpetuate ill-feeling and freshen the recollections of much that had better be forgotten.

Let me add a few words regarding the fate of some who have figured in my story. The Rev. Steele Dickson spent years in banishment. His sufferings were terrible, but he lived to record them, and to be restored to the bosom of his family. He died in poverty and lies buried in a pauper's grave in Clifton Street, Belfast. His tomb, however, has recently been marked by a suitable monument. Jamey Dillon, the scoundrel who betrayed Warwick, found it impossible to live at Drumawhey in conequence of the odium in which he was held. He removed to the town of Donaghadee, and there built a house, the cost of which was defrayed by Warwick's blood money. To the present day the street in which he built the house is known as " Warwick Street." Here, too, he found life insupportable. Leaving that place, he went to the townland of Ballyhay, which is about a mile from Donaghadee, and lodged with a relative there. When he appeared in public he was shunned by the old and hooted by the young. For a long time previous to his death he sat by the fireside, refusing to go to bed, so horrible were his dreams of the night. Dillon is dead, but his evil deeds will never be forgotten.

Ill fortune seemed to follow all who acted a base part in those troublous times, from Dillon, the publican, to Lord Castlereagh, who died by his own hand, in popular ignominy.

The Rev. Robert Black, a Presbyterian clergyman of Down, afterwards of Derry, was base enough to act as a Government spy and receive emoluments for the information he supplied. So degraded did he afterwards become in the estimation of his brother clerics and the public that his mind appeared affected. He ultimately committed suicide by leaping from Derry Bridge into the river Foyle.

Good old widow Warwick, having mourned for years the murder of her son, passed away from earth. Their ashes mingle in the same grave ; their spirits are united in the Better Land.

Merry-hearted Mat M'Clenaghan lived to a good old age. Some of his descendants still reside in the Ards, and one of them pursuing the calling of his predecessor. May he never find it necessary to imitate Mat's example in forging pikes !

The participators in the scenes of '98 have passed away. History should deal fearlessly with them ; the present generation should speak reverently of them. Through all time fathers and mothers shall tell to their offspring the mournful story of

BETSY GRAY,

AND THE BRAVE HEARTS OF DOWN.

[THE END.]

W. G. LYTTLE, 1844-1896.

In the grounds of Bangor Abbey, in a secluded corner adjacent to the Newtownards road, there stands a memorial to the author of Betsy Gray. It reads:

"...a man of rare natural gifts, he raised himself to a high position among the journalists of Ireland. He was a brilliant and graceful writer, a true humourist and an accomplished poet. Robin was a kind friend, a genial companion and a true son of County Down."

An accountant, a teacher of shorthand, an elocutionist and, in later years, a newspaper editor, Wesley Greenhill Lyttle was above all an entertainer, often in the guise of his alter-ego "Robin", a jovial country farmer who regaled his audiences in Ulster-Scots.[1] Lyttle had been a lecturer in Dr Corry's *Irish Diorama* company which toured Britain and America with a show entitled `Ireland, its scenery, music and antiquities'. The show featured large limelight views of Irish beauty spots, illustrated in prose, verse and song. For most of the 1870s Lyttle lived in Belfast where he began to write and perform his humorous monologues. However, he took a change of direction in 1880 when he established the *North Down Herald* in Newtownards. In his first editorial he claimed that the paper would be independent, " `devoid of party politics, of an aggressive nature, we shall know no man.' He proceeded to quote from Gilbert & Sullivan's 1878 triumph *HMS Pinafore*; Sir Joseph Porter always `voted at his party's call, and never thought of thinking for himself at all.' There are no Sir Joseph Porters on the staff of the North Down Herald."

Lyttle moved the newspaper to Bangor in 1883 and had it assume the additional title of *The Bangor Gazette*. As editor, he allowed his imagination to enhance his reports. On occasion the usual matter-of-fact style would give way to humorous accounts of cases from the local magistrates' court. Even totally fictitious happenings could appear, much to the amusement of his friends and consternation of his enemies. A collection of these articles would still be of interest if published today.

Lyttle published his humorous monologues as *Robin's Readings* and continued to give public performances. He staged the first Burns' Night entertainment in Bangor in 1895 with limelight views of Scotland and novelty views of Bangor [Belfast News-Letter, 26th January, 1895].

Undoubtedly, Lyttle's fame today rests largely on his novel Betsy Gray. It first appeared in serial form in the Herald, beginning on Saturday 7th November 1885. Another of Lyttle's serials, *Daft Eddie or the Smugglers of Strangford Lough* appeared in 1889. Serials were popular attractions in

Victorian newspapers and periodicals. Charles Dickens first published his novels in this form. However, a fellow novelist, Mrs Margaret Oliphant, expressed her anxiety over `the violent stimulant of weekly publication with its necessity for frequent and vapid recurrence of piquant incident and startling situation.' In short, the author would include a number of `cliff hangers' to ensure the reader would buy the next issue.

Betsy Gray or, Hearts of Down appeared in paperback in 1888; a third edition came in 1894 and an illustrated sixth edition was published in 1913 by Robert Carswell, revised by the Belfast antiquarian Francis Joseph Bigger [Irish Book Lover, Volume IV, February 1913, page 128].

Lyttle's account of 1798 is not primarily historical, but is rather a melodrama in serial form.[2] *Betsy Gray* was meant to be read by the fireside after a day's work, or aloud to friends and family through the winter of 1885/6 and, if we assume one chapter was printed in each week's issue of the *Herald,* it would have continued until the end of August 1886. Nevertheless, because Lyttle has recorded the traditions from 1798 told at the Six-Road-Ends and Greyabbey areas, his work contains fragments of history not written down elsewhere.

THE LEGEND OF BETSY GRAY

Possibly the first reference to Betsy appeared in Rev. Thomas Ledlie Birch's *Letter from an Irish Emigrant,* written in the autumn of 1798. Describing the aftermath of the Battlle of Ballynahinch, he referred to the killing of `a young [unnamed] woman.' Here we find the legendary Betsy still in embryo. A Dublin newspaper of the day, *The Freeman's Journal,* embroidered its account of the Down rebellion thus: `...to excite them to desperation, these rebels had two standards borne in their ranks by a pair of very handsome women, who were fantastically dressed in green and other silks, one of whom they called the Goddess of Liberty and the other of Reason, both of which unhappy women were shot in the conflict. They were supposed to be women of abandoned character, whom these maddened wretches obliged to assume these characters.' [Freeman's Journal Volume 38, Number 152, Saturday 16th June, 1798]. While it is not at all certain that the report is true, the image of Betsy as standard bearer occurs in later accounts and is picked up by the Nationalist Revival at the end of the nineteenth century.

Betsy's death in battle inspired Mary Balfour, a local Romantic poet (1798-1819), who was probably of an age with her subject. Balfour gave lyrical form to the legend in her poem *Nancy of the Branching Tresses,* published in Hope: *a poetical essay with various other poems* (Belfast, 1810). However, the most detailed account of Betsy at Ballynahinch came from Mary Ann

McCracken. In her old age she assisted R. R. Madden to compile material for his eleven volume work *The United Irishmen: their lives and times*. Of Betsy she wrote:

`Elizabeth Grey, of Killinchy, went to the camp of the people of Ednavady, near Ballinahinch, with some things for her brother and an associate of his who was her sweetheart, on the Saturday before the battle. She remained with him, and determined to share their fate. They procured a pony for her, and thus mounted, she went into action bearing a green flag. On Wednesday, the day of the fight at Ballinahinch, after the people were defeated, she and her friends fled, and on their retreat they were overtaken by a party of the Hillsborough yeomen, within a mile and a half of Hillsborough. The young men were at a little distance from the girl, seeking a place for her to cross the river, and could easily have escaped. But when they saw her in the hands of the yeomen, they ran to her assistance, and endeavoured to prevail on the men to release her, offering themselves as prisoners in her stead. Their entreaties were vain, the girl, her brother, and her lover were murdered on the spot. The two wretches, who perpetrated this brutal act, were Little, and Thomas Neilson, of the parish of Annahilt. The young woman was the first who suffered. Neilson shot her through the right eye, the brother and the lover were then dispatched, and their dead bodies were found and buried by their friends (Little's wife was afterwards seen wearing the girl's earrings and green petticoat). An officer of the regulars came up shortly afterwards with the party, and he reprobated their conduct in the strongest terms. These particulars were communicated to me by a man on whose veracity I could entirely depend, whose friends had been at the battle, and who lived in the neighbourhood of the yeomen.'[3]

THE APOTHEOSIS OF BETSY GRAY

The Irish cultural revival at the end of the nineteenth century swept up the Betsy Gray story as reinvented by Lyttle. In 1896 Alice Milligan and Anna Johnston founded the nationalist journal *Shan Van Vocht* (1896-99). Johnston was a prolific writer and Betsy Gray soon became `Ireland's Joan of Arc', metamorphosing into a model for all Irish nationalist women, rather different from Lyttle's idealized domestic angel. Betsy had become a Hibernian Bellona, goddess of war:

`In the hottest and most glorious part of the fight when Munro led his intrepid pikemen to the very muzzles of the English guns, Betsy Grey, mounted on her splendid charger, and dressed in green silk and brandishing her light and brightly burnished sword, rode by the side of the general leading the faithful hearts of Down. In the desperate and victorious charge... where the chivalrous Monroe and the dauntless and beautiful maiden (for if tradition be correct, there was no fairer face in Ireland) led, who could fail to follow?' [Shan Van Vocht 1896, Volume 1. Pages 97-98]. This is, perhaps, a Betsy more attuned to the end of the nineteenth century when women such as Johnston were defining an active role for themselves, just as the Suffragettes were about to do.

The grave of Betsy at Ballycreen, near Ballynahinch formed a focus for nationalist activism, for visiting and speech making. Anna Johnston's reinvention of Betsy Gray coincided with the centenary of the 1798 rebellion and the item on Betsy in the Shan Van Vocht encouraged the formation of Betsy Gray '98 clubs, and also a Matt McClenaghan club as part of the United Irish League. The highlight of the centenary was a parade in Dublin which included a northern contingent almost 2000 strong, led by Joe Devlin. `Betsy Gray' also appeared in the parade, dressed in green and gold. The clubs bore banners depicting notable figures and events from 1798 as well as, arguably, the very first United Irishman, St. Patrick [Freeman's Journal, 16th August, 1898, page 4].

This `greening' of Betsy Gray naturally caused resentment among those who relished the story but who rejected the Home Rule and separatist movements. Confrontation and conflict over the possession of the story resulted in the swift demolition of the monument recently built in her memory at Ballycreen.[4] As a loyalist apologist for the demolition of the pillar put it, `local Protestants were inflamed because it was organized by Roman Catholics and other Home Rulers. They didn't like these people claiming Betsy...' [Betsy Gray, Mourne Observer edition, 1968, page 163].

But not only Roman Catholics claimed Betsy. A United Irish remnant still remained in the hills of North Down, most notably at Moneyreagh, among the Non-Subscribing Presbyterians, led by the Rev. Richard Lyttle (no relation to W. G. Lyttle).

The story underwent further transformation in the period before the 1916 rising, this time for the stage. In Patrick J. Bourke's melodrama *For the Land She Loved* (1915) the characters from Lyttle's novel were amalgamated with the storyline of another '98 novel, Margaret T. Pender's *The Green Cockade* (1898). Written primarily for a Dublin audience, the Ulster-Scots of Lyttle gave way to the speech patterns of the South of Ireland. Bourke employed the usual tropes of melodrama, a villain, abduction, murder, daring escape, duels, including one between Betsy and a female loyalist rival, culminating in the Battle of Ballynahinch and Betsy's emergence as Ireland's Joan of Arc:

Betsy Gray: Yes it is the duty of every Irishwoman... to rally round the flag to strike for liberty. It is now breaking day. I understand you are to attack the town at day break and now I want to warn you that I shall be ready, mounted on my pony, waiting to join your ranks as you pass along to attack the town.

Battle and fire opens.

Betsy Gray: He that dares to fight for Ireland let him follow me.

All cheer. End of Scene.

Bourke wrote and produced plays on different historical themes and Betsy's last line here quoted is probably a reminiscence from a ballad about another Ninety-Eighter, Mary Doyle the heroine of Ross, who in William Rooney's ballad of that name declares:

"Whoso dares to die for Ireland, let him come and follow me!"

Since the bicentenary of the rebellion various studies have considered the role of loyalist and republican women in 1798. Other `Betsys' have emerged. In addition to Mary Doyle, in county Meath the story of Molly Weston tells of her riding into battle on a white horse and perishing with her brothers at Tara.

Betsy Gray's story grew from a brief reference as a camp follower in an early account of the Battle of Ballynahinch, through poems, ballads, serials and plays into a mythical figure who now haunts the romantic imagination. One pilgrim to her grave described the effect on him of the romance of this tradition:

"I went history book in hand, to the spot and invoked her spirit. She was obliging and stood by me for a brief moment in her green uniform and white cockade, the jewel-hilted rapier in her hand… I wonder why Ulster has never raised a monument to her name, or does she prefer the quiet hawthorn hedge, blackbird and thrush of her native Down, whose corn she once bound into stooks upon her father's farm?"[5]

The monument he sought will always be W. G. Lyttle's novel.

Kenneth Robinson

NOTES

1 His name is usually given as Wesley Guard Lyttle, an error first committed in the obituary published in the Belfast News-Letter, Monday 2nd November, 1896. However, the probate of Lyttle's will and published legal notices name him as Wesley Greenhill Lyttle. The error possibly arose from a confusion with the prominent Methodist of the day, Rev. Wesley Guard.

2 For a survey of the sources Lyttle used when writing Betsy Gray, see

K. Robinson Betsy Gray Revisited in The Journal of the Upper Ards Historical Society 24 (2000), pages 8-13.

3 R. R. Madden - Antrim and Down in '98: the lives of Henry Joy McCracken, James Hope et al., page 244. For a discussion of Betsy's provenance, whether Killinchy or Ballygrainey, see Jack McCoy, Ulster's Joan of Arc: an examination of the Betsy Gray Story, Bangor, 1989.

4 See McCoy, op. cit. for the row over Betsy's grave.

5 Denis O'Donoghue Hanna: The Face of Ulster, 1952, page 124.

BIBLIOGRAPHY

Cheryl Herr , *For the Land they loved: Irish Political Melodrama,* 1890-1925, Syracuse University Press, 1991.

Daire Keogh & N. Furlong (eds.), *The Women of 1798,* Four Courts Press, 1998.

Rolf & Magda Loeber, *A Guide to Irish Fiction 1650-1900,* Four Courts Press, 2006 (it lists Lyttle's publications).

Eileen Reilly, `*Rebel Muse and Spouse: the female in '98 fiction' in Eire-Ireland* 34 (2), 1999, pages 135-154.

THE AUTHOR

Kenneth Robinson is the author of *North Down and Ards* in 1798 (1998) and has edited Thomas Ledlie Birch's *Letter from an Irish Emigrant* (2005) and *William Sampson's Memoirs* (2007), published by Athol Books.

Other titles in the Ulster-Scots-Classics Series:

1. *The Scot in Ulster* by John Harrison

2. *Sons of the Sod* by W. G. Lyttle

3. *The Scot in America and the Ulster Scot* by Whitelaw Reid

The Ullans Press is the imprint of The Ulster-Scots Language Society, formed in 1992 for the protection and promotion of the Ulster-Scots language. It encourages the use of Ulster-Scots in both speech and writing in all areas of life.

For details of how to become a member of the Society and support us in our aims, please feel free to contact us:

The Ulster-Scots Language Society
68-72 Great Victoria Street
Belfast
BT2 7BB
Telephone: 028 90 436716
Email: usls@ulster-scots.com
Website: www.ulsterscotslanguage.com